IRON
in the blood

Four decades on the railways, from graduate
trainee to managing director

RICHARD MORRIS

IRON
in the blood

MEMOIRS

Cirencester

Published by Memoirs

MEMOIRS
PUBLISHING

25 Market Place, Cirencester, Gloucestershire, GL7 2NX
info@memoirsbooks.co.uk www.memoirspublishing.com

Printed in England

CONTENTS

This book is dedicated to

Sarah, Tom and Catie

and to the memory of Thomas Morris (1915-2003)

ACKNOWLEDGEMENTS

I am very grateful to the following people:

Pat Howlett for assisting with the typing and advice

Nick Ambrose for encouragement and advice

My wife Sarah and my family for putting up with me talking about
the book every day for months

Chris Newton of Memoirs Publishing for encouragement and advice
and for editing the manuscript

The Railway Children charity for the good work they do

Finally, to all the railway men and railway women I have met.

INTRODUCTION

I have written this book to celebrate the challenge and the fun I have had working for the railways for 42 years. It is an acknowledgement of many wonderful colleagues and some of the more humorous events that have happened to me. It covers the three decades from 1970-1999, finishing as I left Eurotunnel and ventured back into privatised railways.

Although I have not discussed this in detail, it is well known among my colleagues that while I had nothing against the privatisation of the railways I do take issue with the nonsensical organisation that it has spawned. It is interesting that the wheel is beginning to turn full circle and that soon, I believe, we will revert back to some of the old principles which have remained constant and true.

I also take issue with some of the personnel who came into the railway at privatisation, thought they knew best, did not listen to those who did and made some basic mistakes that affected the industry for years.

Having said that, privatisation had its advantages. If only we in the nationalised railway had had the backing, both financial and political, that the privatised railway has, we would have been far better off.

This book is not meant as an erudite and learned study of railway management, nor is it focused on the equipment the railway uses. It concentrates on the railway's most valuable asset - its people.

I have provided character sketches of many of my colleagues. I have deliberately set these in alphabetical order, in groups between the main chapters. I would apologise to anyone I have left out and trust they will forgive me. Some of the characters are from a time frame after 1999.

There are many people to thank who have encouraged me and helped me to put the book together; Pat Howlett for her constant advice and help, Nick Ambrose for corrections and suggestions and of course all railway men and railway women for affording me the opportunity to work with such a wonderful group of people.

I am delighted too that all profit will be donated to the Railway Children Fund. I can remember clearly the enthusiasm and dedication that David Maidment displayed when he started the fund. It has grown, as it should, into a powerful charity that is doing much good. I hope this book will both give enjoyment as well as helping the railway children.

CHAPTER 1

APPLICATION

When I was directed into Miss Peacock's office, because Cluedo was in vogue at the time, I wondered as I waited to see her whether she might have been doing something wicked with Colonel Mustard in the Dining Room. I hope her reputation did not suffer much as a result of the Waddingtons character.

When I was finally summoned, she shimmered at me, gorgeously radiant and appropriately dressed in blue.

'Do you know what you want to do?' she enquired, somewhat apprehensively. The apprehension was born, I am sure, of inexperience of the world she was being called to advise upon. Careers departments were in their infancy and pitifully inadequate. Miss Peacock was in luck with me - no need for any advice.

'Yes' I said. 'I want to join British Railways on their graduate training scheme.' Miss Peacock visibly relaxed.

* * * * *

It was 1969 and I was entering my third and final year at Exeter University, studying for an honours degree in Classics. The connection between Classics and the railways may not be immediately apparent. Suffice it to say that my headmaster had said that a good classicist can do anything.

From an academic viewpoint, a Classics degree provides a good grounding in employing a reasoned and balanced approach to issues

1

and assists greatly in employing a logical method of problem solving. Thus I believe that its recipients are admirably suited to a career in general management. I recall that the majority of my friends thought that I would either teach (which I did, for a year) or take up holy orders (which I did not). That was a common view of the prospects for a classical scholar. People were always surprised when I outlined my intended career.

I had attended University College School in Hampstead from 1957, and having developed a modest talent for Latin and Greek, I elected to take those subjects at A level along with Ancient History. I have always been more of an 'artist' than a 'scientist', as my science master would have undoubtedly confirmed.

I was privileged to have been taught at A level by two scholarly, learned and inspiring teachers who were rated among the best in the country. If teaching could be measured by results, they would certainly have been at the top of their profession. Their record in guiding boys to Oxbridge exhibitions and scholarships remains unparalleled. Over 100 were awarded during the 30 years they taught together. In their last year of teaching together, eight boys took the exams and all were awarded scholarships.

Dr Usher and Aubrey Morley cajoled, persuaded, motivated, inspired and entertained me through the three years to A level, at which I achieved modest success. I was the only one from the classical upper sixth to read Classics at university and obtain a degree in the subject. That sounds impressive, until you realise that other degree successes from my form included Persian, Icelandic and even Architecture. These two teachers were to me as Dr Arnold was to Tom Brown. They were brilliant scholars who practised the true meaning of 'education' - to draw out. It is not about cramming in. I owe them both much.

My family had been involved in the railway industry for three generations before me. I had worked on the railway as a summer job. At the age of 15 I worked as a messenger at 222 Marylebone Road, the BRB HQ (now the Landmark Hotel). I was known as the 'greyhound', because people there said that when they called for me to come to their office, I was there before they had replaced the telephone in its cradle.

This speed was to be my undoing. I ran round a corner on one occasion straight into the august and rather portly figure of Dr Beeching, Chairman of the Board, and knocked all the files he was carrying out of his hand. He rightly ticked me off, and I helped him to pick the papers up and replace them in the files. Someone later suggested that the closures the great and good Doctor imposed were probably never intended, as I had put the stations to be kept open in the 'to be closed' file and vice versa.

In following years I worked on the seat reservation telephone booking lines at Euston, both the old and the new stations. Our job was to receive requests from travel agents and book the reservations by circling the seats on a chart for each train. The charts would be made up into tickets and dispatched to the travel agent. My only claim to fame there involved, at the request of the other operators, answering the phones for 15 minutes, each call in a different accent, while they listened in!

My father joined the Great Western Railway in 1930 as a goods clerk. Despite leaving school at the age of 15, the gown of scholarship sat easily upon his shoulders. He was self-taught. Combining an impressive intelligence, magnetic personality, innate charm and an unparalleled sense of humour, he was selected to be a trainee manager and progressed through the management chain, working mainly within the freight arm of the railway. He broke his service during the war years serving in the Grenadier Guards, was commissioned into the Gloucestershire regiment and saw active

3

service with the 52nd Lowland Division through Holland and Belgium, crossing the Rhine with Churchill – literally - into the heart of Germany itself. Following the war, after a short re-acquaintance with the railway, he became Transport Manager at Cherry Blossom, the boot polish manufacturers, based at the now-closed factory in Chiswick, West London.

When British Rail developed the Road Railer project - a project where lorries were placed on flatbed wagons and carried long distances by rail - he was invited back to the railway. The project was never the success it originally promised, but when containerisation came to the fore he helped to establish Freightliner and became its Marketing Manager. His proudest boast of those times was when he secured the contract with the Royal Household to transport their luggage by Freightliner container to Balmoral for the annual holiday. He finished his career as District Manager Bristol for National Carriers, the road haulage arm of the railway at that time. He was the finest man I have ever met, or ever will.

Mother's father was a guard at Cheltenham St James. She approached Dad's father, who was station master at Ross on Wye, to see if he could help in obtaining a position for my mother on the railway. Dad was brought into the search and Mother was duly appointed to a secretarial position. She originally thought that Dad 'thought a lot of himself'. They became engaged, however, and were married in 1942.

Mother was a typist of exceptional speed and passed all her secretarial exams without dropping a mark. I still have the distinction certificates stating this. She would have maintained a most efficient office, being a first-class administrator and organiser.

Both my grandfathers completed 50 years of service. My great grandfather had already achieved this milestone, having joined the Cambrian railway and worked as chief clerk at Oswestry. My maternal grandfather, Sid Chamberlain, when I first knew him, was a passenger guard at Cheltenham St James. In the tradition of those days, he was extremely smart and always wore a buttonhole, which he would often remove from some poor person's garden on the way to work! Because of heart problems he finished his career at Cheltenham Malvern Road as a ticket collector. I spent many holidays with him riding in the brake van, watching the line ahead through the periscope located there, which allowed the guard to read the signals.

Sometimes I was allowed to travel on the footplate of the Cheltenham Flyer - what a memory. When he went to Malvern Road I accompanied him for his shift and helped him collect the tickets. I learned much from him about the rules and regulations and the culture and language of the railway. These lessons stood me in good stead during my career.

My paternal grandfather, T E R (Tom) Morris, joined the Cambrian Railway at Oswestry, later moving to Cirencester Watermoor on the Midland South Western Junction Railway, where he became stationmaster on promotion. He moved again to Cinderford, Bilson Junction, in the Forest of Dean as stationmaster in 1925. His last position was station master, Ross on Wye, where he retired in 1948, the year of my birth. Ironically he died on the very day that the last passenger train left Ross.

He was somewhat shy and retiring, a man who kept himself to himself, but he was renowned among railway historians as an expert on the tram roads that were the forerunners of the railways. He had a passion for railway history and imparted his knowledge in a series of beautifully-crafted articles in Locomotive Magazine in the 1930s on the subject of the tram roads in the Forest. His work is profusely quoted in H W Paar's books on the Severn and Wye railway and Great Western in Dean.

He was an expert too on the Crimean War, and received letters from all over the world from scholars consulting his theories and knowledge. He left school at 13 years of age and helped support his family of 11 siblings.

My aunt was a guard on the Bilson to Newnham service during the war, and my uncle on my mother's side worked for many years in the booking office at Gloucester.

Iron in the blood; choice of occupation for me almost naturally selected!

* * * * *

I could never be described as a railway enthusiast. I had the Ian Allan books and dutifully underlined numbers, but I was never quite sure why! I love the industry for its people, its diversity. The sense of service is, surprisingly to some outsiders, very strong, although I do feel this is diminishing. Above all I have so enjoyed the fun I have had.

I submitted my application and awaited the result. The first hurdle to be crossed in the race for acceptance took the form of a formal meeting at Exeter with a railway manager, a Mr Parker, who was assigned to the university for the purpose of making an initial selection. I spent about 20 minutes with him. The subject matter was wide and diverse. I enjoyed the interview, unprepared as I was. This lack of preparation was born of my ignorance of how to prepare or what to say, through a lack of any advice at school or university.

I should point out that although I mentioned my father's association with the railway during the interview, I am convinced no nepotism took place and I am certain no strings were pulled. Clearly my background helped, for I was able to converse on railway matters with some ease, but it would never have occurred to my father to exert any pressure at all.

Following this preliminary interview, I learned that I had been shortlisted to attend a further series of interviews to be held in a lodge in Windsor Great Park (at that time owned by British Rail). If the lodge itself was as romantic as it sounds, it had an even better surprise to offer. It was the training ground for chefs who aspired to positions on the restaurant cars and British Transport Hotels, which at the time were a part of the overall railway organisation. Thus, while career aspirations remained unfulfilled for some - the inner man was certainly satisfied.

The selection process took four distinct phases. First, one's social graces were tested. Because of the length of the selection process, it was necessary for candidates to stay at the Lodge overnight. This gave the opportunity for selectors to observe behaviour and conversational and social skills, particularly during dinner. I was placed on a table next to one of the selectors.

On discovering that I had worked during my holidays at Euston - both old and new – this man questioned me closely regarding the design advantages of the recently-remodelled terminus. Anxious to demonstrate a critical mind that could identify problem areas, I held forth at some length to the assembled company how I believed the planners of the new station had been deficient to no small degree. Youthful exuberance ran away with me. How ridiculous, I pontificated, to put the mainline platforms at the two extremities of the station, thus causing problems when queues formed for the booking office or the shops at the edges of the concourse and blocked people trying to leave or join main line services.

Confident that my audience was hooked, I warmed to my task. I further stated with an air of enforced nonchalance that the planner had obviously understood nothing about railway operations and in my view should be dismissed from the service. I finished my harangue with this somewhat draconian uttering and I awaited reaction.

I began to sense that all was not well, for the other diners were staring in embarrassed silence at their plates and there was a chill in the air. The railway official fixed me with a steely glare.

'My name is Mr Leppington' he said. 'I was in charge of the project!'

Lemmings, cliffs and jumping came to mind. Humour can help. I rearranged my knife and fork, stood up and remarked that I would ask the reception to order a taxi. Mr Leppington disagreed and suggested I resume my place. Inexperience and lack of diplomacy had nearly cost me my career - as it was to do on many occasions later.

The second part of the process was taken up with a précis exercise and an intelligence test. During the latter, we manfully struggled to decide whether the next in the series of pictures had three arms or four legs or which shapes followed which. I never have, nor ever will, see the point of such tests and have long wondered whether the people who design them are merely confidence tricksters more concerned with making an easy buck than scientific analysis. Certainly I have never encountered a situation where the tests carried out were re-examined after, say, one year of employment, to see how accurate they were.

The next section of the day was taken up with a series of one-to-one interviews, each with a different manager. I can only recall one of them in any detail, Mr Rupert Shervington the then Divisional Manager at Kings Cross. He told me in a gruff military bark to 'siddown' and asked me only one question, in stilted staccato tones reminiscent of Mr Jingle from Pickwick Papers. The analogy must end there, for he was anything but flighty - he was a 'man's man'.

'Chap told to do something. Won't do it, refuses. What do you do?' he barked.

Management theory, such as I knew it, piled upon management

theory in my mind. Motivational techniques, conversations with human behaviourists from my college days, discussions with psychology students, experiences I had had, all these thoughts cascaded into my mind.

Rupert glared at me. 'Well?' he roared.

'I think I would ask him why he wouldn't do it' I stammered unconvincingly.

'Nonsense!' came the reply. 'Only one way, son. Kick him up the arse and tell him to get on with it. Now get out!'

He pointed to the door, and I thankfully and with alacrity put myself the other side of it, licking my wounds. I was now convinced I had blown it completely.

The last part of the day was given over to group discussion. Like King Arthur's knights, we sat round a table. One poor blighter was given the chairman's job. Around the room sat the observers and interviewers. Such a technique of selection, I believe, is effective but cruel. Obviously your sentiments and intentions are firmly fixed on one goal, and that is to impose yourself by systematically destroying the opposition, ie the other candidates, in a gentlemanly way. I cannot recall the subject under discussion. The observers sat with an air of excited indifference, occasionally making notes. I would love to see those notes now.

Eventually the gladiators were stood down by the referee and we were allowed to go our separate ways. I emerged into Windsor Great Park with a vacuous feeling. I was uncertain whether I had done my best because I was uncertain what I had been supposed to do - I had no benchmark. I was also curious to know what the railway felt they had learned about me as a person, what my ideas and ideals were, what made me tick, whether I fitted into the required profile. I did not feel particularly tested, nor had my intelligence been stretched.

* * * * *

Casting my mind back to my schooldays, my career guidance was virtually nil. This was surprising, given that my school was so progressive in many other ways. I think we had a careers section in the library, but I never found it. My future, post-university, was never discussed. The school was not just intent on gaining university places for its alumni, as it had been founded on very different educational principles. Scant attention, however, was paid to the choice of a career. There was no careers master, and when they did appoint one after I had left he was shunted into the position and had no real interest in the subject. It was not the personalities who were at fault but the system, particularly the lack of foresight.

Thankfully, times have changed. There is now a strong realisation that the subject is important, and a high degree of professionalism and resource has been allotted to it. When I departed from the school and following the appointment of the first careers master, the school carried out a volte-face. Aubrey Morley, my Classics master, was asked to carry out the task, and he typically attacked the issue with a cocktail of thoroughness, enthusiasm and empathy. He established the department virtually from scratch. He visited different companies, the better to understand the qualities that were sought and the type of work on offer. He spent time with me at Tinsley in Sheffield when I was Area Manager. He watched, listened, debated and questioned all he met. He impressed them all too, particularly, I recall, the ASLEF union representative. It was nothing more than I would have expected from such an enlightened, intelligent and urbane man.

As a result of his visit and success, I introduced a series of secondments for local schoolteachers to the area and carried on the practice elsewhere. The three-week secondments offered the opportunity to experience all aspects of railway life. The secondees attended during holidays, and judging by their reaction they felt the process to be worthwhile and of great assistance.

Companies must play their part in this process and offer the opportunities to teachers and pupils alike. Work experience is a good vehicle, if properly planned and implemented. If we do not invest in our youth we are facing an uncertain future.

* * * * *

During the interview process, which culminated in the offer of a place on the railway training scheme, I had been asked if I wished to state a preference for a location during the 18-month period, should I be successful. I had offered no preference and was assigned to Liverpool Street Division, part of the Eastern Region. On informing my father of the intended training ground, he, being a staunch supporter of the school of thought that the 'Great' in Great Western Railway was put there for good reason, asked disparagingly, 'where's that?'

I discovered later that several of my future colleagues had stated preferences, and in the true tradition of British Rail had been placed at the opposite end of the corner of the network from their choice. I little realised at the time how lucky I had been. In retrospect I could not have had a more varied and interesting division in which to learn my craft.

The railways at the time were organised under the umbrella of the British Railways Board into five regions; London Midland, Eastern, Southern, Western and Scottish. Each region was subdivided into divisions. The Eastern region at the time had nine divisions, including Liverpool Street. The divisions were further divided into areas, although on the Eastern and Southern regions some of the areas were managed by station managers. The tradition of station managers or station masters continued in the Southern region long after other regions had abolished them in favour of areas. The difference between the two was normally size related.

The areas managed traditional operating staff, signalmen, shunters and guards and also included booking office staff or freight clerks and the associated commercial activities. In the early seventies on the Eastern, drivers were managed by depot managers who reported through the mechanical engineering line. Civil engineer staff, signal and telecommunications, overhead line staff and their depots were all managed through their discipline and were co-ordinated at the lowest point at divisional level under the divisional manager.

The organisation was based on the principle that at divisional level and above there would be a general manager, while the professionalism of each discipline would be maintained by reporting through the particular discipline's hierarchy. Thus the Regional Operating Manager would hold the professional responsibility for rules and regulations etc through the divisional operating manager to the area operating manager.

The area/station managers too in the Eastern region reported through the Divisional Operations Manager, emphasising the perceived importance of the operating railway at the time. The regional general managers were powerful 'barons'. While it is axiomatic that some were more successful than others, the calibre of the occupants was high and they provided a focal point - a leadership. Everyone was well aware who was in charge. Their decisions were based on consideration of the arguments from all persuasions and backgrounds, and the decisions were founded therefore on their experience.

Who is in charge now? Where is the collective wisdom? The

answers to those questions provide the key to the sad state of the railways today. No one is in charge - there is little or no collective wisdom.

* * * * *

The Liverpool Street Division incorporated an interesting mix of traffic. The major passenger flows were commuter traffic into and out of Liverpool Street from Essex, Norfolk, Suffolk, Hertfordshire and Cambridgeshire, the London Tilbury and Southend (LTS) line from Shoeburyness into Fenchurch Street and some smaller passenger lines, Stratford to North Woolwich, Stratford to Tottenham and part of the Barking to Gospel Oak line. The main line formed the Intercity service to Norwich, but only as far as the section between Manningtree and Ipswich, where the trains were handed over to the Norwich division.

Freight was well represented also by container traffic from Felixstowe and Thameside and marshalling yards at Temple Mills and Ripple Lane, the latter almost alongside the huge Ford car plant at Dagenham and a fair amount of oil tonnage from depots at Purfleet and Thames Haven. There was a large variety of local traffic around the division, with traffic as diverse as animal feed into a depot at the back of Thornton's fields carriage sidings, furniture into Witham, steel into Sanders and Fosters sidings at Stratford, export and import traffic into and from Poplar Dock - a railway-owned dock which had originally been owned by the Great Western railway, cullet (broken glass) to Manor Park and even rotting fish, which was transported in open wagons through Temple Mills to be converted into fertiliser. This gave the seagulls a good meal and gave the staff at Temple Mills an instant laxative.

There were major depots at Stratford, Ripple Lane and

Colchester for locomotives and electrical multiple unit depots at Ilford Car Sheds, East Ham, Southend and Clacton. The only major type of traction capability that was absent was the third rail (where electricity is picked up by the train from a conductor rail at ground level) with most of the railway being powered by 25kv with the Electrical Controls at Romford and Pitsea.

LEW ADAMS

In 1971 I had completed a project as a management trainee that involved using a minibus to transfer drivers on weekend engineering work between the depot and the site of work for relief purposes. Traditionally walking time was paid and rewards were high. I was proposing a large reduction by scheduling a minibus to carry out the task. The Divisional Operating Manager, Brian Driver, had instructed me to put the project into effect and as such I had to meet the ASLEF Union representatives from Stratford, the local departmental committee (LDC) to put my proposals to them.

This was a bit like approaching Herod to ask him to be a godfather, and I was terrified. The reputation of the LDC was frightening and none more so than a certain Lew Adams, originally a Cambridge man, who had stamped his mark on Stratford depot and whose repartee and ability to think on his feet were legendary.

Mr Frank Heslop, Depot Manager, accompanied me at the meeting and protected me. Actually the LDC was very restrained. They asked me some difficult questions and probed some of my arguments but the meeting was conducted in a polite and positive way. This, I found out, was ASLEF's way.

Lew remained a gentleman to me for the rest of his career. He was elected General Secretary for the union and carried out his task with great professionalism. Not everyone agreed with him, but he was always courteous and firm.

Present at that meeting was Tony West, who also joined the Executive with Lew. They were a formidable pair.

Lew was asked to be a non-executive member of the SRA under Sir Alastair Morton. On arrival at his first meeting Sir Alastair introduced us, though he knew we were old acquaintances.

'Do you remember,' said Lew, 'when we were at Stratford, I called you governor?'

'I do,' I replied.

'Now that I'm on this board,' said Lew,' you f****** call me Sir.'

For once Sir Alastair was lost for words.

Lew was elected out of office and in my view his union did him a great disservice. He had guided the union through the privatisation and through extremely skilful negotiation had left the RMT light years behind and secured a very good deal for his members. Skilful, highly intelligent and quick on his feet, Lew was a formidable negotiator and a total railwayman.

JAMES ADESHIYAN

I met James when I worked with London Lines. Sartorially elegant with a wonderful smile, he was the Route Director for Great Northern. He was a delight to work with. Very professional in his approach he possessed that wonderful quality - the wish to learn. He had come to the railway from Tie Rack, where he had been a sales executive. Clearly his appearance would have been important in that job, and he maintained the habit.

He was a great customer champion and had an eye for detail. He also made sure that his staff practised the highest standards. He particularly shone in the aftermath of the Potters Bar accident. He arrived on site and took care of all the passengers on the train with great empathy and professionalism.

I introduced him on one occasion to a member of the National Express Board, who asked his background. On being told he had worked for Tie Rack, the Board member asked James what he thought of his tie. It was a particularly bland affair and I feared for what James would say. I need not have bothered. 'It makes a statement,' he replied. I wish I was that quick!

NICK AMBROSE

Nick works in the field of safety, which in itself can be a barrier to fame. Everyone thinks they know how to manage safety and some regard the whole issue as an annoying irritant that stops them doing their job.

In order to manage safety one needs to be professional, patient, extremely polite, very knowledgeable, witty and balanced, and above all be able to demonstrate empathy. Enter Nick, who demonstrates all these qualities admirably and as a result is very successful at what he does.

I first met Nick at Chiltern Railways, where he was fighting a battle against some indifference rather than outright hostility. He was beginning to win through, however, and to make his mark. I like to think I helped him raise safety awareness, but most of it was down to his character and drive.

I shall remember Nick particularly for his engaging sense of humour and his slightly quaint love affair with the stories of Sherlock Holmes and other like pieces of literature, and our shared fascination with every detailed fact and snippet associated with President Kennedy's assassination.

A classic incident for which Nick has been teased mercilessly occurred when we worked for Crossrail. He was thoroughly confused about station signing in the event of working 'wrong road'. We were discussing the difficulties with a train in the tunnels working single line and entering a platform from the wrong direction. Seeing a slightly troubled look on his face, I asked him if anything was troubling him.

'We would have to change or duplicate all the exit signs' said Nick. 'Otherwise passengers would not be able to see where the exits were.'

We could not make him see that there was no problem, until someone pretended to get off the train and walk backwards and the penny dropped.

The importance of having a good safety manager is paramount. It is often a position that is feted when an initial appointment is made, until the new occupant of the post puts their foot down over an issue that could affect a bonus or a reputation. Then the fine words can be forgotten. That is when a company needs a Nick to be responsible for safety, for someone like him will always find a way through the problem and arrive at the right answer.

Nick joined me at Eurostar and within days had established his credentials through a wonderful cocktail of charm and knowledge. He is a great colleague. In safety and in operational matters a combination of the science and the art is all important. Nick has that in abundance - a lovely man.

KEN BRITTON

'I hate management trainees' came the opening gambit. 'Make me a cup of tea.' I duly produced the tea and Ken stared at it for some time. 'Fetch me a pair of scissors' he said through gritted teeth.

'Why scissors?' came the incredulous question.' To cut the top off the f****** cup. Next time fill the bloody thing up.'

As a management trainee one paid visits to every type of office and operation that the railway delivered. Some locations were eagerly anticipated, others were looked on with apprehension. One such location was Temple Mills marshalling yard in Leyton, East London. On my arrival I met Ken Britton, who was the senior AYM - assistant yard manager. The AYMs worked on shifts, the senior one deputising as necessary for the Yard Manager.

Ken was an ex-Petty Officer, Royal Navy. He was a very capable manager with a very good brain who had almost stifled his own advancement through his difficulty in managing upwards. He had a bag of chips on his shoulder and was unable to suffer fools gladly for a nanosecond.

From this poor start, our relationship could only go up, and up it went. We became firm friends and I learned much from him. He had a way with words, delivered in a Somerset/Dorset border drawl. Making a point, he would sometimes say,' I'll bet you a penny to a bunch of s***, and you can hold the stakes in your mouth.'

My favourite was used often, and particularly when I had become Yard Manager. During our daily morning conference I would ask a question about the operation of the yard the previous day. Ken would eye me wickedly - I could have written the script. 'Far be it from me to criticise my governor, not having had the benefit of a public school education...'

Ken retired from Temple Mills. He was capable of a lot more, in or out of the industry. I know the railway tried to assist his career, but he would have none of it. I also know that more effort should have been made, as he was in the top drawer of railway operators and much loved by his staff.

The Kens of this world are few and far between now and the world is a poorer place for that. I was always so glad I had been able to establish good and meaningful contact with him. Goodness knows what he would have said if he could have read that last sentence!

My paternal grandfather at Cirencester Watermoor. My father is
sitting on the wall in the middle.

GLOUCESTERSHIRE RAILWAY STATION STAFFS.
No. 1. CIRENCESTER M. & S.W.J.R. STATION.

Back row:—Signalman Miles, Porter Harris, Foreman Cole, Porter Ockwell, Porter Smith, A. S. Hinks, and W. J. Perrott.
Sitting: T. E. B. Morris, F. W. Dunford (Station Master), W. G. Maslin.

My grandfather in a staff photo (front left)

My maternal grandfather at Malvern Road, shepherding
schoolchildren on to a train

My maternal grandfather, front left (note the buttonhole)

Extn. 5683.

R.J. Morris, Esq.,
6 Highfield Way,
Rickmansworth,
Herts.

74-102-70   20 March 1970.

Dear Mr. Morris,

Following your meeting with the Central Selection Committee, I
am glad to tell you that we can offer you an appointment under
our Management Training Scheme. I should be grateful if you
would let me know whether you wish to accept.

I enclose a note which gives details of the conditions of
service which cover these appointments. The salary is £ 1050
per annum in the first year of training and £1100 per annum in
the second year. plus £50 per annum graduate allowance.

The appointment is subject to a satisfactory medical examination
by one of our Medical Officers, and to your obtaining your degree.
I shall want you to tell me in due course the result of your
final examinations.

The normal starting date for the training is the beginning of
September. When I hear from you that you wish to accept the
appointment, I will arrange for you to meet the officers who will
be responsible for your training, and ask them to settle with you
the date of your medical examination, and the details of your
appointment.

Yours sincerely,

DIRECTOR OF MANAGEMENT DEVELOPMENT.

My letter of appointment, 1970

Temple Mills marshalling yard from the control tower,
looking towards the hump

My friend Mike Jones in
Room 97A Hamilton
House, Liverpool Street
divisional office

Making a retirement presentation to Harry Faulkener

Open day at Tinsley Yard

On the radio while Area Manager at Tinsley

Receiving a leaving presentation from the staff at Tinsley –
Frank Seeds to my right

CHAPTER 2

TRAINING

The 34 trainees of the total 1970 management trainee intake were divided for their training locations into the five regions and each was allocated a division, either individually or in pairs. Eight trainees were sent to the Eastern region, two to Liverpool Street, two to King's Cross, two to Leeds and two to Newcastle.

Trainees were a mixture of staff entrants and graduates. I can safely say that I never experienced any indication that any discrimination was either felt or practised by either. I believe we fed off each other's experiences and benefited through our contact. Interestingly, and indeed uniquely, the eight trainees on the Eastern region were all graduates. Of those eight, I had the pleasure of working with Mike Donnelly at Eurotunnel 23 years later, with John Wilson when he worked for Network Rail at Liverpool Street when I was working at West Anglia Great Northern Railways (WAGN) and with Richard Goldson when we worked together at National Express.

Three trainees left fairly quickly after their training. There is a latent bond between trainees of the same year's intake. Chris Leah, who was a London Midland trainee worked closely with me when I was Chairman of the Institution of Railway Operators and he was the deputy chairman. It was an association I valued and one that was made easier by our 'history'.

My partner at Liverpool Street was David Cruttenden. David was a huge man who had rowed for Cambridge in two boat races, the second as the President. I tried my best, for obvious reasons, not to upset David. On one memorable occasion my left-wing views contrasted with his, which leaned more to the right. In desperation he tore the telephone directory in half. I left the room quickly.

The training consisted of a Cook's tour of British Railways, visiting area, divisional and regional offices in all departments interspersed with a variety of courses at Derby training school on management techniques and lectures from the great and good. As one would expect, the experiences varied from intense interest and stimulation to complete boredom and indifference (both on my part and that of the teachers). In essence, however, it was a worthwhile and fascinating experience and went a long way to preparing us for our first appointments. I felt at the end of my training that I had had a good grounding in most of the aspects of the freight and passenger railway, both in operations, commercial and engineering terms.

The training was, of course, a mixture of theory and practice. While theory is, of course necessary and important, it was the practical aspects that attracted me most. During training, therefore, it was the periods spent in the signal boxes, in the marshalling yards and on the footplate that I particularly enjoyed, since it gave me the hands-on experience. There can be no substitute for training and awareness of this kind. No one can understand an business like the railway industry unless they have 'felt' it. The present privatised railway has introduced a cadre of managers who cannot boast these skills, and some do not even think them important. The railway is the poorer for it.

Just as in the forces the sergeant-major or equivalent is vital to the smooth functioning of the regiment, so the divisional and regional inspectorate were the hub around which everything revolved. The main operating departments were the traction, signalling, passenger and freight inspectorates. Liverpool Street division was blessed with a particularly professional and competent complement.

David and I spent two weeks with the traction inspectors. Tony Oughton, Bill Brown, John Jarvis and Ken Mayhew made us particularly welcome and willingly imparted their immense knowledge and experience as best they could in the time available. I attended a day's traction training at Ilford training school - a place which reminded me of a Portakabin Dotheboys Hall. I was introduced there to such mysteries as the triple valve (not easy for one who dismally failed Science 'O' level), and nodded sagely through lectures on the air brake. I undertook footplate rides, which included driving a Type 47 [the diesel locomotive type used to haul passenger trains to Norwich] from Stowmarket to Diss with Bill in close attendance. I even managed to stop at Diss in almost the correct place. These experiences added considerably to my knowledge and confidence. Sadly Bill will not read these words, as he died all too young not long after our training with him.

Room 61 of the then Hamilton House, of which there is now no sign, was the home of the Divisional Signalling Inspectorate. The Chief Signalling Inspector was, in my view, as near to God as man can get. It was said of Charlie Coleman that he had no need of the Isle of Wight ferry - he just walked across. I have met many professional people in my life but there are two who stand out. Both were Divisional Signalling Inspectors, Coleman and Chief Inspector Forrester at Bristol. Both feature in the character sketches. Their knowledge of rules and regulations was complete, their standards were of the highest order and their presence was commanding.

The signalling inspectorate was a uniquely talented and hospitable team. Ken Pumfrey, the assistant chief and a member of the Magic Circle, proved a very able deputy. I have always been fascinated by magic, and the combination of professionalism in his two skills made Ken a personable and interesting colleague. Cyril Harris, who always sported an impish grin and was well versed in the industry, was well able to impart the tricks of his trade. Arthur Barnes, who was responsible for the London Tilbury and Southend line, was a man who needed convincing that you were of the right calibre. Once that respect had been earned a lifetime's experience was on offer and genuinely shared.

Wilf Raleigh was genuinely helpful too, and patient at explaining and, on many occasions, re-explaining, complex signalling issues to those who showed a penchant for learning.

Inspectors were designated to passenger and freight activities. Archie Green always seemed to be around. His job was to chase performance through identifying problem areas in the passenger railway and offering solutions. He was popular everywhere and had that rare gift of remaining so while stamping his authority when necessary. Jack Durrell was the freight inspector, who remained optimistic and cheerful while moving through a less clear world of freight wagons, shunting poles and brake sprags. With his help I learned much about loading and train preparation, all of which stood me in good stead in my early career. George Taylor, the Signalling Inspector for the West Anglia lines, seemed not to like me, and we avoided each other.

I took great pleasure in the many discussions about rules and regulations that took place at all hours in Room 61. It was a tremendous way to learn my trade, and I was encouraged by the Inspectorate to visit as often as possible to take part. Indeed, I travelled with Charlie regularly from Chelmsford to Liverpool Street and would spend journeys talking on related subjects on many occasions. Charlie would, on quite a few occasions on arrival at Liverpool Street, follow a traveller who had travelled in our first class compartment to the ticket barrier. As the unwitting soul showed his ticket, Charlie would pounce triumphantly and challenge him or her to the effect that they had been travelling in a first class compartment with a second class ticket. An excess fare would be issued. I was always amazed that he was invariably correct at spotting a defrauder. He eventually let me into his secret. 'Look at the shoes,' he advised. 'If they're clean they're first, if not they're second'.

* * * * *

Another practical element of our training was in the control office. A railway control, I have discovered, is an activity little known outside railway circles. Most lay people believe that the signal boxes are the only method of control. They forget that an organisation as logistically complex as the railway demands an all-seeing eye to look over it. Train crew allocation, stock or resource control and running decisions were taken in the control office. The office also assumed command during major 'perturbations of the service', which ranged from derailments to major accidents. Each division possessed a control overseen by a regional control, in the Eastern Region's case in York, while the British Railways Board also managed a countrywide control office. Each control assumed more strategic and less tactical decisions the higher it was in the chain.

Liverpool Street control in 1970 was divided into six running sections, plus a train crew control, locomotive control and an assistant general purpose controller. A Deputy Chief Controller (DCC) maintained overall supervision, assisted by an assistant, who was responsible for freight movements. These teams worked seven days a week, with a slightly diminished complement at weekends and on nights. They were present on Christmas Day even after the decision was taken to run no trains. They were needed because the overhead line was energised, even during Christmas

Day, and the control were the coordinators between the electrical control and the signalmen.

The six sections, or tables as they were referred to, were as follows: Liverpool Street and its environs as far as Bethnal Green; Bethnal Green to Shenfield and Southend; The Lee valley as far as Bishops Stortford; Shenfield to Clacton, Walton and Manningtree; the London Tilbury and Southend Railway; and finally the freight area around Temple Mills and the North London Line. There were bordering control offices at Kings Cross, Cambridge and Norwich, with a link on the North London line to the London Midland Region.

The office was a source of a great wealth of knowledge, for most of the staff had spent almost all their railway careers in control. This was due partly to the interest factor but mainly, I fear, to the money trap. Controllers' wages were embellished by overtime and rest day working, and many a good manager was forced into remaining there, not realising their full potential.

Liverpool Street Control was never dull. There was always something to sort out, ranging between major and minor, and every crisis demanded a solution that might be both intricate and time-consuming. This was particularly true of the train crew controller. He seemed to me to require the qualities of Solomon, combining consummate diplomacy when trying to persuade crews to do what he wanted with the ability to gamble on an immense scale and the wisdom to look into the future when making plans and promises. It was his job to ensure that whenever crews were displaced they were manipulated back on to their diagrams (or schedules) as soon as possible to maintain adherence to the plan. It was of no surprise to me that John Muffett, who was a train crew controller, was also the Control chess champion.

In times of crisis, senior management tended to gravitate

24

towards control offices. The unfortunate DCC often found himself briefing six managers in succession. Some were genuinely interested in helping to sort out the problem. Some wanted to know if their train home was running. Others paced around the office peering over controllers' shoulders and occasionally asking what could be regarded to the uninitiated as erudite questions. Many were fatuous, born of a need to impress; the glorification of the uninvolved.

Decisions taken in the control office could affect performance very easily, for the results of poor controlling could remain for some time after an incident had been closed. I well remember my good friend Mike Jones, now a director of Hull trains, deciding to detrain a Harwich loco-hauled boat train at Goodmayes in the middle of the evening peak. His plan was to transfer the passengers cross-platform to another train. He had overlooked the problem of luggage and forgotten that there was a bridge with no lift facilities that had to be traversed to reach the other platform. Couple to this the fact there were very few staff on duty at Goodmayes and all the ingredients for a disaster were in the mixing bowl.

Both lines were blocked for about an hour as long-suffering passengers struggled over the bridge with heavy suitcases. The evening peak was completely ruined. I know Mike will not mind me recounting the story, as we still laugh about it now - not at the expense of the passengers, I hasten to add.

The staff in the control office displayed a dogged attitude to the business of keeping the railway going. Given the number of incidents requiring our attention, they also displayed a remarkable fortitude in keeping at it in the face of sometimes insuperable odds.

* * * * *

I have referred to the need for knowledge of the rules and

regulations by which the railway operates. It was obligatory for all management trainees to learn and to be examined in them to the highest level.

Eight weeks were spent at the Derby school to learn the theory. After four weeks, there was practical training in the field. The whole course culminated in an eight-hour oral examination with the regional Signalling Inspector at York – about on a par with a visit to the dentist. I was told at the beginning of the exam that I would be allowed two mistakes!

Part of the practical training involved working shifts in a signal box to observe and learn the signalling part of the regulations. I was assigned to Wickford signal box, between Shenfield and Southend. The box controlled the main line and the junction of the single line from Southminster. At 09.00 on the first day I walked off the down platform country end, in a downpour as I recall, over the up line (no red or green zones then) and mounted the steps to the signal box. I opened the door and stepped in hesitatingly.

'And who might you be?' asked the signalman.

'Richard Morris, management trainee' I replied.

'Can you read?' He barked. 'There is a sign on the door. It says 'private', so get yourself outside and knock on the door'. I withdrew hurt, and knocked. Over the next five minutes the rain found its way into every gap in my raincoat, and I resembled someone who had taken a shower fully clothed. Eventually I heard a call of 'Come in' and entered, to steam gently by the stove.

The signalman's name was Wally Trigg and he was 65 when I met him. He eventually retired at the age of 80 as crossing keeper at Mucking Crossing on the LT and S. To the day he left the railway he cycled to work - sometimes long distances - as he was a relief man and worked many signal boxes and crossings.

'Why are you here?' he demanded.

'To learn about signalling' I squelched.

'One way to learn - do the job.' He sat down on the bench at the back of the box, pulled his cap over his eyes and appeared to nod off.

I started well. The bell codes and the simple signalling on the up and down lines were within my compass. Then a bell sounded which indicated that a train was ready to come off the single line from Southminster and required access to the up bay at Wickford.

It is possible to work out the sequence of operating the levers to accomplish moves by examining the block diagram which hung above the frame and showed the layout with all point and signal numbers. The plates attached to each of the levers indicated the levers that would have to be operated before that particular lever could be moved, or come out of the frame. For instance, to pull a point lever which had a lock on it, the lever that operated the lock would need to be operated first to 'unlock' the points concerned. Before the signal controlling that move could be operated, the points, once moved, would need relocking. The facing point lock number would therefore be on the plate of the point lever, and both would be on the signal lever

The levers were coloured differently to denote their different functions: red for home signals, yellow for distant signals, black for points, blue for facing point locks etc. I started to set the road and made good progress, until the inevitable happened - one lever would not come out of the frame. I rechecked the sequence. I thought I had got it right. I glanced at Wally. He remained in a somnolent posture. I tried again, to no avail. The DMU off the branch came to a stand and whistled. What was I to do?

'Pull number 18 and then try again' said a gruff voice behind me. His cap was still over his eyes. I did as instructed and the road was set.

'Right, young 'un' said Wally, 'I think I can make a signalman out of you.' I had passed the test. I was accepted. What a piece of luck that Wally did accept me, for he taught me much, and I enjoyed my three weeks with him.

He had a habit of bringing a sponge cake to work with him. The first time he asked me if I wanted some, I watched in horror as he cut the cake into two huge slabs and gave me one. I was more specific with future requests. He did explain to me that if he were to return home with any cake, his wife would regard this as an insult and would never bake one for him again.

Management trainees, especially graduate trainees, were frequently regarded with disdain, particularly among the supervisory cadre. Following training, a trainee would be placed in a grade 'C' or 'D' position, sometimes without interview. The tradition of seniority was very prevalent in the railway, and many found it difficult to accept that after many years of service they were passed over for a 'whiz kid', particularly one from university. I met some antagonism, though I was shielded somewhat by my family history. I always made sure colleagues knew of my background early in our acquaintance.

One of the worst places for such prejudice was Temple Mills. Some examples of this are contained elsewhere. 'The Mills' was situated just northeast of Stratford and was a major marshalling yard dealing with wagon load traffic. Freight was divided between wagon and block load traffic. The former was basically individual consignments and could range, as I have stated, over a large range of goods. Block load or train load traffic involved the whole train comprising the same commodity travelling in one 'block' from origin to destination without the need for splitting or division. Probably the two best examples are oil and coal, designated as 'merry-go-round' travelling for colliery to power station.

Jim Wilson was the yard manager when I did my training. He was an amiable Scot who had been worn down by the difficulties of running the yard, for it was always fraught with industrial relations and staff problems. He made sure David and I received a good grounding in how things worked. There was something logical about the operation of marshalling yards that appealed to me, and could explain why I spent much of my time associated with them.

* * * * *

Several courses were held in the railway school of transport at Derby. This establishment was designed in the art deco style and had some delightful features. It was a bit run down, but served its purpose. Its principal was Leslie James, a tall bespectacled man who had stepped from a Dickens novel. He had held some high office connected with the law, and maintained the air of a barrister prosecuting assiduously. He delivered one lecture (and only one) to a series of trainees on the subject of internal controls. He emphasised how important it was to maintain a close watch on all matters financial and stated that in his opinion it was one of the most important elements of successful management.

His credibility was destroyed, however, when it was found that the bursar at the school had systematically, and over many years, milked the school's finances to his own personal gain. I think the lecture was dropped from the syllabus after that - or maybe the deliverer of the lecture.

Each trainee had to sit at top table once during their visit to the school. When my turn came I found myself next to the Divisional Operating Manger of the Nottingham division. I had been on the railway about three months and he asked me how many engineering possessions (when work on the track is carried out, so called because the engineer takes possession of the line) I had been out on at the weekends.

'None' I innocently replied.

'You should eat, sleep and drink railways' he said. 'If you had displayed that sort of lack of commitment and I had interviewed you I would not have taken you on'.

'If you had said I had to act like that I would never have joined!' I retorted. I was summoned to Mr James' office and warned as to my future conduct. I took no notice then and never have since!

I have found that in any course or lecture that I have attended, there are one or two points that stand out in my memory and are inspirational in changing ideas or the processes by which I have managed. One such incident occurred during our training at Derby. Each trainee in turn would be designated to meet and greet any visiting speaker and introduce his or her lecture - good practice for future years. John Wilson had the honour on this particular occasion. The lecture was due to start at 09.00, but by 09.15 there was no sign of John or the speaker and we began to fidget.

The two of them appeared about 20 minutes late. The speaker looked in a sorry state; hair ruffled and tie not straight. Worst of all, his flies were undone. John introduced him as a speaker on the subject of passenger marketing.

The gentleman stood up and thanked Mr Heath (sic) for his introduction (think politics of the time here) and questioned the subject of the lecture. 'I've got it down as freight marketing' he said. John assured him it was passenger marketing. 'Have to think of something to say' said our speaker, who was rapidly losing our goodwill.

Not an auspicious start. Late, ignorant of the chairman's name, unkempt and unprepared. Suddenly he turned on us. 'What do you think of me?' he asked. We went through the list and he, through this brave ruse, taught us how important preparation is and how important to success. He restarted the lecture in a more fitting manner, and I have remembered his message.

The school at Derby was a microcosm of the institutionalised railway - it was run, and felt like, an institution. The highlight of every course was the Thursday visit to the Cock at Ripley, where we concentrated on points and curves of a different nature. We felt like naughty sixth formers boarding the bus.

* * * * *

Part of the training programme involved the undertaking of a project. As always, there was a strong emphasis on cost savings. I was given the task of recommending train crew savings measures during weekends, particularly in the area of crew relief to trains which were required to remain on site, sometimes all weekend, and how it could be made more efficient. Ballast, or engineering trains, would set out on Saturdays to all points on the division and would require train crew relief as they could remain on site until Monday morning in some cases. Because of the difficult geographical locations in which the work took place, train crew were able to book huge amounts of 'walking time' from the nearest railway/public location. Many of them used their own cars to get to the site and thus were able to book time for an activity not carried out.

I had the idea of diagramming a minibus which would travel to and from the depots at Ripple Lane, Temple Mills and Stratford taking new crews to site and collecting those being relieved. The project found some favour with the management and I was asked to take three weeks away from the scheme and implement the idea. This involved meeting the Local Departmental Committees

(LDCs), who were the union representatives at local level, in order that the matter might be consulted upon. The theory was that consultation was like marriage, ie you did as you were told; negotiation allowed some discussion and did not need to be necessarily accepted. If a 'failed to agree' was registered, the issue would be elevated to the regional level at Sectional Council.

I knew the LDC at Temple Mills - for some unfathomable reason they called me 'the Prince'. Now I had to meet ASLEF in the persons of the Stratford LDC. Lew Adams was the chairman and Tony West the secretary. Their reputation was fearsome. I have to admit to being very nervous. In fact they were very firm but absolutely fair - I think they treated me kindly. I was to get to know both of them far better in my later career when they were both elected to the National Executive of the Trades Union. Tony was the loveable rogue, Lew the voice of reason. Neither of them ever broke an agreement they had made, and I count both as good colleagues.

In retrospect I enjoyed the training period more than I thought I was doing at the time. I appreciated the companionship of other trainees, and I believe I succeeded in establishing a good rapport with most of the staff I met, which resulted in my learning a great deal.

The time had come for my first appointment. I was summoned to the office of Brian Driver, the divisional operating manager, to discuss my placement. There were two jobs on offer, an assistant station manager's post, grade D, at Ilford and an assistant yard manager's post, grade C, at Temple Mills. The Temple Mills job was therefore junior. David Cruttenden had already opted for the Ilford job. As I have said he was a huge man. He was appointed to Ilford. but I had a problem. I did not wish to go to Temple Mills.

Mr Driver asked why not. 'Because it's dirty' I stammered unconvincingly. 'Then clean it up!' said the unimpressed divisional operating manager.

He explained the benefit I would derive from such a post. I would be thrown in at the deep end of man management in particular and I would become very quickly acquainted with the basics of railway operation. I grudgingly accepted his advice and went to Temple Mills. I believed he was wrong. I soon found out he was absolutely correct. I learned my trade quickly and I loved working there.

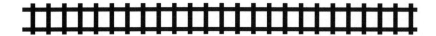

ROY CALVERT

This man had the most influence on my life on the railway. I met him first at Liverpool Street, when he arrived as Divisional Operating Manager from the Beckenham division of the Southern Region. The angel of fate was looking kindly on me that day. I was an operating assistant whose job it was to work closely with the DOM. I could not have had a better mentor or teacher.

He, I believe, knew that he was suffering form an incurable form of leukaemia and paid regular visits to hospital in his native Geordie land. As a result he lived life at great speed and lived it to the full. We all worked hard, learned hard, drank hard and laughed hard.

Roy had an amazing ability to understand when he was not getting through and adapted his approach accordingly. He was, in the words of my father, a good man whose values were worn on his sleeve. Above all he was a tremendous leader and motivator who used his tremendous operating capabilities to inspire and excite.

On one occasion, after he had taken me to Tinsley, I was winding points at Aldwarke Junction, a particularly difficult junction to operate manually, having a double scissors. It was snowing and bitterly cold. After I had been there for about two hours and feeling as if I was seizing up, I heard a shout of 'Richard!' It was Roy.

'Thought you would like a flask of soup,' he said. No soup has ever tasted better. What a piece of motivational management.

Roy's personality and drive infected the division from his first day. He injected a 'can-do' attitude and certainly was not prepared for a second-rate response to a crisis. His success in revitalising the division was down to the fact that he had a great talent for operating and understood the job so well - there was no argument, he was usually right.

He combined that professionalism with a wonderful zest for life and a great sense of fun. We played cricket on one occasion against a local Chelmsford team, and since I had organised it I was appointed captain. Roy was the wicket keeper and as the first delivery slid past me at cover point, I made off to chase it. My ears were assailed with shouts of 'come on' – 'hard in' – 'keeper's end', etc. I threw the ball in and at the end of the over suggested to Roy that the way I played cricket did not fit with shouts and gesticulations. Roy looked at me. 'Today, you are in charge. Monday morning, I am in charge.' I let him shout.

When Roy left the Liverpool Street division and went to be Divisional Manager Sheffield, he appointed me to Area Manager Tinsley. This was difficult for him as I went up two grades, and worse than that I was a southerner going north. He had absolutely no doubt that he wanted me to go and that is what he got. It was ever thus with Roy.

Only once did I see him become really annoyed. The area managers in the division had a regular meeting with him. Roy had issued an edict that on a particular date he wanted some specific information.

'Have you all got the letter?' he asked. We all said we had. One of our colleagues, however, became brave. 'I have got it here' he said, 'and do you know what I am going to do with it?' He was assured we didn't, though foreboding filled the air. With that he screwed it up and threw it over his shoulder. Man is but mortal, and all of us became concerned. Roy took the gentleman next door and for about 10 minutes the walls of the office bowed inwards and outwards. We sat in silence, thinking of nothing else other than how we would provide the necessary information.

Roy's funeral was conducted in Sheffield Cathedral on a day when the snow seemed determined to keep everyone away. Chris Daughton and I skidded our way to the service. The cathedral was full, the tributes glowing.

Roy Calvert demanded high standards of professionalism and was truly inspiring. He was lost far too young, but though I have worked with many very good operators, I have never worked with a better one. I owe him so much.

ARTHUR CATHERALL

Arthur was small in stature, but he made up for it with a hugely interesting personality. He had a disarming way of looking at you when you were speaking, with his head slightly tilted on one side and a very piercing look in his eye. He had another disarming habit; he could jump from a standing start and with one bound jump from the floor to the top of his desk.

Arthur was the Divisional Movements Manager at Bristol when I was appointed his assistant. My imminent arrival must have adversely affected him, for on the day before I started he suffered a serious heart attack and was absent for the first few months of my working there.

Arthur would be particularly remembered by those who spent any time with him for his love of Rommel and his hatred of Mrs Thatcher. Most situations encountered either by Arthur, or more particularly by others, would have been solved, in Arthur's view, by Rommel or a division of panzers. During dinner in the mess, he would employ the salt and pepper pots, sauce bottles and cutlery, even your own when you were trying to eat, into describing Rommel's battle plans. His knowledge was outstanding, his loyalty to Rommel's abilities total.

His feelings towards Mrs Thatcher proved more embarrassing, for he would regale anyone who would listen, and usually those who did not want to listen but were forced to by their proximity, on what an evil woman she was. One such peroration took place on a bus in Bristol, when I was forced to protect him from pounding umbrellas wielded by angry middle-aged ladies.

Arthur was a very good railwayman and an extremely kind and emotional man. If ever you had a problem, Arthur would listen and help if he could. We both struggled with the individual who was the Divisional Manager at Bristol, and Arthur helped me come to terms with his difficult approach to management. The Divisional Manager left not long after my association with him, proving how accurate cockney rhyming slang is by becoming a merchant banker.

Arthur's heart never really recovered from the initial attack and he too died a relatively young man. He brought much to the railway and to all who worked with him. Perhaps his main gift was the hint of eccentricity which endeared him for his difference. I admired that, but I remember him particularly for his kind counsel.

CLEM CHAPMAN

I don't think my father ever forgave me for working on the Great Eastern, being a Great Western man through and through. I had my first taste of working on the 'Western', as it was then, at Bristol as Divisional Movements Manager. I quickly realised why the Western had the reputation it enjoyed.

Early in my time there, I decided to go Exeter to revisit old haunts. Clem Chapman was the Divisional Signalling Inspector, and it was his duty to meet me from the train and conduct me 'round the patch'. On arrival I spied an extremely smart railwayman, standing to attention with the old brown Western cap badge , no longer in use, resplendent. I walked over to him and the salute he delivered would have pleased my father, an ex Grenadier guardsman.

Clem had a broad Devon accent which was delivered at a high level of decibels. Extremely smart, always deferential, he really epitomised the old pride and the old order. His driving, however, was something else. South Devon passed as a blur. No sooner had I recognised one village than we were in the next, all the while to the accompaniment of Clem's rich tones. He was a man who spoke with his hands too, which did nothing for my pulse rate.

We arrived in a cloud of dust at Paignton and proceeded to approach the signal box. To my horror I saw a plate-layer sitting in the box as we approached. I knew there would be trouble, but I was not prepared for Clem's reaction. He began to snort audibly and twitch visibly. On opening the door I knew the poor man was doomed, for he was tucking into a plate of bacon and eggs and all the trimmings.

Clem roared. He picked up the breakfast and threw it out of the box. He then picked up the plate-layer and threw him out too. Both landed at the bottom of the box steps. Clem proceeded in colourful tones to remind the unfortunate wretch that signal boxes were not for eating breakfast in, a message he relayed to the signalman and to most of the populace of Paignton. He then turned to me and in hushed and reverential tones apologised and sought my understanding.

Perhaps Clem was a little too eccentric, but he was an intensely proud man whose sole purpose in life was to do a good job to the very best of his abilities. He brooked no reduction in standards. We could do with a few more Clems to balance much of what I see today. I certainly raised my 'bar' as a result of meeting him.

JIM CLAXTON

My lasting image of Jim, who is almost 2 metres tall and a huge man, occurred in Japan. We were representing Crossrail on a visit to Hitachi's factory to gain an idea of their capabilities and ethos to help us prepare a tender for the new rolling stock to operate the service.

We had not learned early enough that if you empty your plate in Japan they will just fill it up again. Jim's appetite was akin to that of Desperate Dan from the Dandy comic. If you took him to one of the 'eat all you like' restaurants, the owners would be very quickly bankrupted.

We were in a station restaurant sitting in front of huge plates of noodles with napkins the size of tablecloths wrapped around our necks. We had eaten two bowls and I had given up. Jim finished four, and became a hero to the Japanese in the restaurant and to the waiters, who were awestruck. He was applauded from the room. Big man, big appetite, huge heart and gargantuan intellect.

We had met at Chiltern and I quickly realised Jim was in the wrong job. He was head of drivers - he had been a driver himself - and was doing a good job, but I could see he had untapped qualities.

I needed someone to create an operational strategy, someone who could think out of the box. Jim seemed to possess those gifts and I asked him if he would like to be Operations Strategy Manager. I thought he would be good, but I did not know how good. He is brilliant at thinking strategies through and proved an extremely loyal deputy. It was a good example of taking a calculated gamble and on this occasion getting it completely right.

When I transferred from Chiltern to Crossrail I was keen to engage Jim as soon as possible, and appointed him Railway Production Manager. We had three more great years together before he moved on to Network Rail as part of their Crossrail team.

I have often been faced with the problem of listening to a presentation or reading a document and finding it either difficult to understand the import of the words or having nothing particular to say. Jim could always find the angle and always seemed to ask the right question. His output too was well thought through and valuable. His standing as a result within the industry has grown considerably and it is much deserved.

Two things not many people know about Jim. He has a degree in biology (as does his lovely wife Wendy) and he played in a pop group with the unlikely name of the Waving Daisies. One of the best men I have worked with.

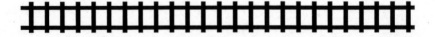

CHAPTER 3

TEMPLE MILLS

The Temple Mills marshalling yard was north of Stratford, close to Leyton underground station. It covered a huge area, including Temple Mills Works adjacent to it, which had once been a full works involved in locomotive construction. When I went there in 1971, the works carried out wagon repairs only.

The yard had been modernised in 1958 at a cost of £3.5m as part of the wagonload improvement programme. Not only was it enlarged but a hump was installed to recognise the increased throughput the yard would accommodate. The hump allowed wagons to roll by gravity towards the main yard and into the correct road for their ongoing destination. Effectively it was a very large bump. Locomotives pushed the wagons up one side, and because they were uncoupled they would roll down the other.

The derivation of the name 'Temple Mills' - always a rather grandiose name, I thought - is worth a explanation. In medieval times the area was almost entirely rural. Arable crops were grown - beans, wheat, oats and barley. The need for grinding the grain for bread spawned several mills. The Temple Mills were water mills belonging to the Knights Templar, who used them to grind the corn grown in nearby Homerton. Their mills straddled the River Lee.

The 17th and 18th centuries saw a variety of processes being carried out on the site. Rapeseed was ground for oil, leather was produced, brass kettles were made, yarn was twisted and lead manufactured. Even gunpowder was produced in the area; an explosion in 1690 killed several people, including a French minister. In the 19ᵗʰ century the mills were demolished and the land was used for railway purposes to accommodate the expansion from Stratford.

The yard was divided into six parts, Reception, West Yard, Manor End, Manor Yard, Departure Sidings, East Yard. Trains would arrive on the reception roads at the north end of the yard, either from Temple Mills West signal box direction or from the Stratford direction. There were twelve reception roads. Once the incoming train had berthed, the locomotive would be released to take up its next working.

Originally, before train consists (lists of all the wagons on the track with their loads and destinations) were introduced, a 'cutter' would be dispatched to walk down the train examining the wagon labels to ascertain the destination of each wagon. He would then 'cut' or uncouple the wagons into their allocation for the main yard. The maximum number of wagons in one cut was six. The main yard road would be chalked on to the leading wagon of the cut, so that the operator on the hump top would be able to set the road to allow the wagon or wagons to be directed into the correct road.

Once train consists were introduced, the cutter would take the list down the train, check it for its accuracy and cut the train in the same way. There was no need to chalk wagons any more since the list, amended if necessary, would be given to the hump operator, who used it to allocate the wagons. Eventually, and when I was there, the consist would produce a punched tape that had all the destination codes imprinted on it. This was fed into a machine which would allocate the wagons and set the points automatically for the desired road in the main yard.

The trains were pushed up to the hump top by two class 350 pilot shunting locomotives, referred to as 'mikes' for some reason, coupled together, and both locomotives were double manned. At least that was the theory, though the presence of four members of the footplate fraternity was rare. There were two sets of paired locomotives working at all times except the night shift on Sunday night. With the other pilot engines working in the yard there were over 50 drivers allocated to the Temple Mills link alone.

The early 1970s saw a huge change with the introduction of computer technology to the freight business. It was called TOPS, Total Operating Processing Systems, which held the records of every freight wagon and eventually every locomotive on the system. It was possible to enquire about the whereabouts of every wagon or to monitor downtime spent in locations and for train information in the form of consists to be transmitted through the network and delivered to the hump cabin as the train was leaving its origin point.

Just before the introduction of TOPS, a system of ATI, Advanced Traffic Information, had been used employing telexes of a train consist. Some genius with a brain the size of Africa had developed ATI a stage further by taking the information about incoming services and determining the optimum 'humping' order to ensure as many wagons as possible made their ongoing connections. He called it geometric blocking, and his task to sell it to hard-bitten yard supervisors proved too much for him. The scheme died, strangled at birth. Surely he had chosen the wrong name. He left the yard in tears.

Once the cuts of wagons reached the hump top, they rolled by gravity into the main yard, with the points to the designated road being automatically set. High above the yard sat the retarder operators, one for each side of the yard roads, or fans as they were called. One operator oversaw fans A to D inclusive, the other E to H. The speed and weight of the wagons would be automatically calculated and as the cut of wagons passed through the retarders, primary and secondary, it would be slowed to the correct speed and left to run down into the new destination road. The task of the retarder operators was to correct the retardation if the cuts were running too fast or to remove it if the wagons were running too slowly.

Derailments at this point were all too regular. The most memorable for me was the wagon of liquorice allsorts that overturned and split open. It took me 20 minutes to get to the site, and not a liquorice allsort could be found. All the shops in Leyton sold them at reduced prices for about three weeks!

The retarders were operated by air pressure and took the form of long clamps which, when activated, would be applied to the wheels of the wagons in the same manner as disc brakes on a car. The noise made by the retarder activation through the release of air pressure was quite loud, and it was a favourite trick of the operators, if they saw someone new to the yard, particularly at night, to give a short blast as the visitor walked past. The reaction of the poor victim was usually both instant and dramatic. The retarder operator would smile benignly and innocently on the unfortunate nervous wreck from his high vantage point.

The maximum number of wagons in a cut was six. Some wagons had 'not to be hump shunted' stencilled on them. There were two main reasons for this. Either the wheelbase was so long that the wagon would rock gently on the hump top, using it as a fulcrum, or dangerous goods were being conveyed. The most dangerous commodities were oil/petrochemicals and, of course, the nuclear flask.

The latter contained a very small amount of nuclear waste in a huge container protected by layers of steel. Its transport around the country caused, and still causes, much angst among some groups, and protests against its carriage were fairly regular, though never at Temple Mills. In order to allay fears once and for all, the BRB decided to stage a collision between a type 37 locomotive and the flask, to show how well it could stand up to such forces. The locomotive was radio controlled of course, and the video showing the test remains quite dramatic. At the time of the exercise, Tom Greaves was the Traction and Train Crew Officer at the Board and we presented him with a cab pass to allow him to travel on the locomotive for that journey only! It remained, framed, on his wall until he retired.

If a long rake of wagons required positioning in the main yard, the pilot engine would remain attached and push them into the required road. If however a cut was being humped into an empty road in the main yard, there was a danger that the wagons could pass straight through the yard and continue to roll unaided towards Stratford. In order to prevent this, wagon chasers were employed. The job they did and they way they did it would give most health and safety experts the urge to lie down for a long while with a very stiff brandy.

The hump supervisor would ask the retarder operator to call, for example, 'empty road Ernie 2', and from a cabin underneath the tower would emerge the 'chaser'. He would identify the cut, and as it left the secondary retarders he would start to run alongside it. He carried a brake sprag with him or a shunting pole, which he would insert into the gap above the handbrake of the leading wagon. It was his job to stop the cut at the London end of the road and pin brakes down so that other wagons could be humped on top of it (or them) as the foundation for setting the road.

The chaser would sit on the pole or sprag and bounce up and down to apply the brakes. The harder he bounced, the more brake was applied. Often the pole would snap, leaving the chaser on the floor and the wagons proceeding on their way. Sometimes the chaser did not respond to the call and an emergency broadcast would be made to warn the London end of the yard that wagons were coming through unchecked. This amazing procedure, as will be seen, was not used at Tinsley because of the method of retardation, but I am not sure what other method could have been used to set an empty road in a conventional marshalling yard other than setting the road from the end opposite to the hump, which was sometimes done.

The main yard consisted of seven fans lettered from A-H and six roads in each fan, except H, which had seven. Fans A and B formed the Manor Yard at the London End, while C-H were designated as the Manor End. Each road therefore was referred to by its alphabetical and numerical identification. The alphabetical tags in the Manor Yard and Manor End were Alfie, Bertie, Charlie, Donald, Ernie, Freddie, Georgie and Harry. Thus the East yard feed road - of which more later - was Ernie 1; the road for wagons needing to go to the workshops (horribly referred to as the 'cripple road') was Donald 6, while the brake van road was Georgie 5. Each destination for services had its own designated road, though there two feed roads in the yard. Ernie 1 and Harry 7 were the feed roads for the East and West Yard respectively. The East Yard made up trains for destinations very local to Temple Mills in East London - Stratford Market, Romford, Silvertown etc. The wagons were collected about twice a shift from the feed road and reshunted over a knuckle – a mini hump - with a ground frame to sort them into their final destination. The West yard operated in the same way, though when I arrived it had closed except for storage of vanfits, the covered traditional railway wagon with doors either side, awaiting the sugar beet season.

Trains which were ready for departure were either drawn up to one of the eight departure roads or left from the Manor End and in some cases the Manor Yard. The Manor Yard formed local trains for the west and north, using a knuckle and a ground frame in the same way as the East Yard, though there was no feed road as the wagons were already in A and B fans. A set of five sidings, the Manor sidings, lay alongside A fan and were often used as departure sidings for the Manor Yard.

Brake vans were humped into one road and shunted to the brake kip, where the tail lamps were fitted and fires lit. When a train was ready it would be drawn clear of the brake kip and the brake van with guard aboard would roll down to the back of the train and attach. The guard would use the handbrake to control the speed.

Sometimes a load would shift when it was shunted or humped. These wagons were taken to the 'cattle dock', where a small transhipment gang reloaded them either on the same wagon or on a replacement. This gang was led by Ron Shann and used a crane that Brunel would have recognised if he had visited the yard. To this day I am amazed how it kept going. It did however usually fail at 13.30 when Ron was due to go home.

The yard humped an average of 3000 wagons per day, though I do remember achieving 4000 on one particularly frenetic day. The system was inefficient, particularly from the cost point of view. The number of staff just involved in the yard itself must have been almost 200. The cost per wagon was very high and took a huge chunk from the 'profit margin' of the transit, if indeed there ever was a profit. Some wagons would have passed through three marshalling yards on their journey, and anything going to Stratford Market, for instance, would be shunted again and another driver and two shunters would transport the wagon - and it could be just one wagon - to its final destination. The system was doomed almost before the modernisation plan was introduced, and it eventually died completely.

I was involved with Temple Mills four times between 1970 and 1977, firstly as a trainee, secondly as Assistant Yard Manager, thirdly as Yard Manager and fourthly as Area Operations Manager Stratford.

As always with the railway it was the characters working there that made it enjoyable. There were three experienced assistant yard managers (AYMs), Jim Lovett, Ken Britton and Ernie Prior, and two younger ones, Mike Anderson and Roy Combes. Ken Britton was the acknowledged leader and spokesman, although Ernie was the official representative.

Reporting to the AYMs, who were responsible for the shift-to-shift running of the yard, were three supervisors, who each had responsibility for one of the sections of the yard, Hump, Manor End and East Yard. In addition a post of supervisor assisted the hump supervisor, with particular reference to the train consist and running information. Latterly, as all the freight management was centred on Temple Mills, a management grade Area Freight Assistant (AFA) was created.

In the administration office, in good old railway tradition, there were two clerks who had fallen out in about 1863 and had not spoken to each other since. All communication between them was through George Dodge, the chief clerk, who had the patience of Job. Jack Fallis made up the complement. At some time Jack had been a fireman and in his mind he had built up a view that there was nothing he could not do. Even the SAS must have consulted Jack before going on a mission.

Guards signed on and off at the yard and these were 'managed' by a guards clerk. The last but by no means least member of the team was Fred Yarham. He had the dubious task of rostering the yard staff and the guards, and he was a consummate chess player. Somehow when all seemed lost for the next week and there were several positions uncovered, Fred would conjure up bodies from nowhere. The trick of course was 12-hour or rest day working. Everyone worked 12 hours and every rest day they could, through some very strange agreements. If for instance a member of the relief staff was rostered eight hours to cover a member of staff who had been asked to cover another turn at 12 hours, the member of the relief staff and the other two members of that roster would all work 12 hours. In other words a 24 hour job would always cost 36 hours. No wonder the wagon load business was doomed.

The top management did not visit the yard very often, but on one occasion I was told that David Bowick, Chief Executive Railways, had expressed a wish to have a look round. These visits were akin to royalty arriving, and I spent some time making sure all would appear efficient and busy. I had reckoned without one thing. George Gladwell was the supervisor on the hump, and George was not the most accommodating railwayman to those who worked at higher levels. I begged him to behave and he promised he would, but the twinkle was in his eye.

I introduced them. 'Mr Bowick, this is supervisor Gladwell, one of our most experienced and competent staff'. Mr Bowick extended his hand. George took it and kept hold of it.

'What do you know about effing marshalling yards?' he said.

Mr Bowick, taken aback, said, 'Well, quite a lot I think'.

'Sit down there' said George, pushing him into a chair. 'Pin your ears back and listen to me for ten minutes and you'll know an effing sight more'.

Luckily Mr Bowick regarded this as his opportunity to say to the Board that he had met some of the difficult staff and had handled the issue well. He must have thought I was some sort of troublemaker, for only about three years after this incident, I was working as the operating assistant at Liverpool Street and we were in the middle of an ASLEF dispute. Mr Bowick paid the division a visit in order to rally the troops and all the Area Managers were invited to the presentation. At Southend the Area Manager was Len Robinson, a lay preacher and one of the most gentlemanly and mild-mannered men you could hope to meet.

Mr Bowick gave the talk purportedly to let us know what the plans at Board level were to solve the dispute and to thank us for our efforts. 'I am sure you would like to ask questions' said Mr Hankins, the Divisional Manager.

Len stood up, and I can recall his exact words to this day. 'When I return to Southend, my assistants will cluster round me to hear the plans and the thinking that is being developed on high at our headquarters in order to solve this dispute' he said. He paused. 'Do you know what I shall tell them?' he demanded of Mr Bowick. The latter assured him he had no idea.

'F*** all' said Len and left the room. The words 'pin' and 'drop' come to mind. None of us had ever heard Len raise his voice, let alone swear. I am sure Mr Bowick recognised that both times he had been insulted in the Liverpool Street Division, I had been present.

* * * * *

Roy Calvert rang me on one occasion and told me the General Manager would be travelling to Tottenham by train and was booked to stop alongside Temple Mills for a briefing. When the train stopped I realised to my horror that there was no shunting to do. I telephoned the Manor Yard and told the chargeman to pull a rake of wagons out of a road over the knuckle and then put them all back again into the same road.

I received a telephone call from Roy later to say the GM had been pleased with the work going on. As I put the phone down

Roy asked, 'Why did you take wagons out and put them back in the same road?'

'Training exercise' I answered.

'Keep thinking like that and I'll make a manager out of you yet' said Roy.

Most of the yard staff were West Indian and delightful. Their one big fault involved dominoes. They loved to play, and they played with venom and force. The dominoes were not placed sedately on the table; they were smashed down with incredible force and resultant noise. Sometimes the only way I could get them to shunt was to steal the double blank.

One of the guards' clerks was Indian. Thursday was payday, and in the summer he had made the error of taking his jacket off and hanging it up with his wage packet in it. Unfortunately it was stolen, and he came to see me in a very agitated state. I started to arrange some remedy for him and went down to see him. Across the mess room doorway I noticed some red powder on the floor.

'What's this?' I asked.

'I put it there' he replied. 'Whoever took my money, if he crosses that line will die.'

After some debate, I told him I would allow him to leave it there for one hour and he would then have to clear it up then. About 45 minutes later, I received a call to say that a driver had been found dead in his car in the car park. He was in his mid-thirties, and had a considerable amount of money in his jacket pocket. The guards clerk insisted the money was his. I treated him very carefully for the remainder of our acquaintance.

When it was payday a crowd of wives would gather round the gate to make sure they were given their money and that it would not be wasted by their husbands. Many staff left by alternative routes, some taking a well-worn path to the bookies. On a few occasions when a member of staff had died and it was my sad duty to visit the widow to put the 'admin' in order, I would take the deceased's last pay packet with me. On presenting it to the widow I would often be met by a gasp of disbelief. 'Is this all one week's pay? I thought it was a lot less!' she would say.

The visits to the bookies did provide one huge advantage, and it took me a long time to realise the connection. Guards and train preparers, as part of their procedures, had to compile a train preparation form to accompany each train. This was carried by the guard and its purpose was to calculate the weight of the train, the brake force and the maximum speed at which the train could run. At that time some wagons were unfitted - that is to say they had no continuous brake pipe that would enable the brakes on that wagon to be applied when applying the train brake from the locomotive. Some trains, designated Class 9 at that time, were entirely unfitted and could only run at very low speeds. This meant that the train could only be stopped by the locomotive brake and could be controlled at the rear - when descending a gradient for instance - by winding the brake up in the brake van. This had the effect of keeping the couplings tight.

If there were some fitted wagons, they would be marshalled at the front of the train and be designated the 'fitted head'. The more fitted wagons, the greater the brake force of the train. The more braked wagons there were the 'lower' the class of train, which affected its maximum speed. Classes 7 and 8 were the other two classes of partially-fitted trains. A train fully fitted with braking on each wagon ran as a class 6.

The calculations were notoriously difficult to achieve and were the bane of many a guard's life. Not, however, if you were used to the intricacies of completing complicated betting slips. Most of the guards at Temple Mills were both adroit and accurate at filling in the information and could achieve the mental arithmetic required with consummate ease.

* * * * *

A marshalling yard could easily seem far from the realities of the business world, since it was rare for freight customers to visit and the operation of a yard could appear mysterious and strange, even to other railwaymen.

The only visitors we did have with any regularity were trespassers. People would use the yard as a short cut, or out of curiosity. Even before the health and safety brigade had cast their malevolent influence over us all we realised that wagons moving silently down roads with no locomotive attached and no one 'looking out' for them would constitute a danger if 'strangers' were in the yard.

Accordingly therefore, on a lovely sunny Saturday morning when I was on duty, I received a call to say that a young couple had been spotted walking in the yard and I immediately issued the instruction to stop humping, an apt word in the circumstances. I summoned as many shunters as I could and sent them off to search individual fans and report back. I said I would search the brake van road myself.

On about the third brake van I climbed on to a huge Queen Mary brake with a massive handbrake wheel that looked like a ship's wheel. I cleaned the grime off the window and peered in. There in front of me was a white backside moving rhythmically up and down. As I opened the door to a mixture of confusion and embarrassment on the part of the young couple, I noticed eight pairs of eyes, wide with excitement, peering in at the other end. The shunters knew where the action would be and were annoyed with me for stopping their Saturday voyeur session.

'Don't ever interrupt in future, guv' they enjoined. 'You'll do someone a mischief!'

We gave the loving couple a cup of tea, probably with condensed milk, which is how we drank it, and saw them on their way. It would not be the embarrassment that kept them away in future but the milk.

I experienced some near misses in the yard, as it was important to remain alert at all times. One such was the result of my own stupidity. We were a staging point for ferry wagons, which, as their name suggests, travelled to the continent on the train ferries. These wagons conjured up pictures of the Second World War and some of its most unsavoury episodes, and had an atmosphere all of their own.

At the end of some of the older ones, a seat had been provided for the guard. It was just a piece of wood positioned on the end of the wagon, and in order to protect the unfortunate man from the elements to a small extent, a roof and sides were provided, but there was no other covering. One summer's night I clambered up to see how it would feel to sit in this position. Uncomfortable as it was, it was hot, I was tired and I went to sleep. My awakening was swift, dramatic and painful. A cut of six loaded ferry vans was being humped on top of the wagon in which I was snoozing. My head banged from side to side on the frame and I very nearly fell off the end, where I would probably have been crushed between the wagons. Lesson learned - I never repeated my folly.

I experienced the 'Mills' in three separate guises; once as a trainee, once as an AYM and once as Yard Manager. It was an experience that still remains clear in my memory as being a tough learning ground but a wonderful experience. As an AYM on my first night turn, the train preparers told me they could not couple up the brake pipes on the Parkeston train. I went to the train and found new 'swan neck' pipes which were attached halfway up the wagons and which, when new, were notorious for having a mind of their own. They were very difficult to join together. It was like trying to force two strong magnets. The train preparers, sadly acknowledging defeat, said they would have to let the train go half loaded and abandon the wagons behind the pipes. They watched me closely.

I ducked under the buffers, held the two clips on the pipes together and let them go. They responded with a satisfying click and joined together. I emerged triumphant. They stood astonished.

'Where did you learn to do that?' one asked.

'My grandad' I answered. 'He was a guard - did 50 years.'

Credentials posted, I was OK from then on. When they found out the other grandfather had done 50 years as well I was almost deified!

Temple Mills closed as a marshalling yard in the 1980s. It remained a derelict site until Eurostar built its depot there and moved from North Pole. Its location is ideal for access to the HS1. I visit there now in my current role and still imagine the noise and the characters-their ghosts live on.

CHRISTIAN COSTA

I have had the good fortune to work closely with many French people and have enjoyed the experience of being stimulated by a different culture. The best of all was Christian. We worked together at Eurotunnel for three or four years and I loved it.

Christian had the appearance of a Mexican bandit. He had a wonderful thick moustache which curled down at the edges. This could have given him a surly look, but because he was always smiling it looked good. Very expressive and demonstrative, he pooled his talents with me, and I like to think we made a good operational bi-national team. We certainly understood each other and agreed on most things.

Christian married a lovely lady who was one of nine sisters. I remember him telling me of the occasion when he first called at the house to escort his then girlfriend to their first date. As he sat waiting in the hall he began to believe he was in wonderland, as through each door that opened appeared another vision of loveliness. He did say in an unguarded moment that he wondered if he had chosen the right one, but I have no doubt that he did; neither has he, I think.

Christian ran the Control Centre at Eurotunnel with a huge helping of discipline, but he certainly turned it into an excellent centre which acquitted itself well. He was an exponent of one of the traits that I have noticed is prevalent among French people - their attention to detail. Nothing escaped him and he would never accept second best. I remember my time with him with great fondness.

DAVID CRUTTENDEN

As trainees we were paired up on the Eastern Region. When I arrived at Derby for the first week of induction I could not help noticing a very tall member of the course who looked extremely athletic, with a huge frame. I have always thought I was tall until I met David Cruttenden (and until my son Tom passed me on his way to 6'7") but he was huge.

David had rowed in two boat races and had been President of the Cambridge boat in the second race in 1969. He had won both races and was horrified to learn that my uncle had gone to Wadham College, Oxford. 'You do know, Morris' he used to say, 'you can smell an Oxford man coming; the only men who wash their hands before they go to the lavatory.' Here was my partner.

I was truly blessed however, for we had a fabulous 18 months together.

I often exasperated him with quasi-socialist babble, and on one occasion in his annoyance he once literally tore a telephone directory in half. I left quickly!

He had a choice vocabulary, using words in unfamiliar contexts. He often talked of someone 'creaming around' and I was often referred to as an 'ace buffoon'. He was, as most huge men are, gentle and soft hearted, and he was the kind of man that would always go out of his way to help if he could. He did not like some of the discipline the railway still practised and would kick against it where he could. He also was ruthless when riled.

There was a Western trainee on the course, Gordon Edwards, who was a mine of information about all aspects of railways. One slightly annoying habit he practised was to talk in railway codes - never coaches, always BSKs, TSOs etc. (BSK meant a brake van, second class corridor coach - K meant corridor.)

One day David announced that he had spotted a KSSB. There was silence in the group. Some didn't care, some were mildly interested, but Gordon was totally hooked.

'I'm not sure I've heard of one of them' he said, slowly musing on the problem. Then suddenly, enlightenment hit him. 'I know! There's only three of them and they have first and second class in the same coach with a corridor that runs down half the coach on one side and then crosses to the other. Fancy you seeing one! Where did you see it?'

David eyed him imperiously. 'In the buffet at Derby station. It's a King-Size Sticky Bun.'

Gordon displayed his railway knowledge less from that time on and eventually, I think, joined the Church. There must be a lesson there somewhere.

We supported each other through some of the more boring times, were excited by the vibrant moments and we laughed and joked our way through the entire programme, never falling out and always enjoying each other's company.

David met a lovely lady named Biffy, who was from Rhodesia. They were married and moved out to what was to become Zimbabwe, so I now see David only occasionally on his visits to this country. I always feel better for meeting him and I always feel good after I have spoken to him for a time. He was a strong man and he still is a strong character, but with that wonderful thick slice of human kindness and love of his fellow man running through him.

CHRIS DAUGHTON

I worked with Chris at Liverpool Street - we were both operating assistants. Chris was a lifelong railwayman who had started at the bottom and finished at the top. He is one of the best organisers I have met, meticulous to a fault. Sometimes his delivery of questions was proof of the man's brain, each word delivered carefully and precisely and demanding precision in reply. 'I – want – to – know', he would intone carefully.

Chris possesses another ability which endeared him to me immediately; he has a fabulous sense of humour and is an incomparable story teller. Some of his tales would have me almost helpless with laughter - such a gift.

We met as families on several occasions and he was just the same. My father always referred to him in glowing terms - no bad accolade. He went on the dizzy heights and it was thoroughly deserved. A one-off.

MIKE DONNELLY

A sandy-haired, beer-loving Novocastrian and a wing forward, Mike was freckled, with a very set jaw when he was feeling obstinate. He joined the railway the same day as me, with a degree in economics. I first saw him on St Pancras station saying goodbye to the lady who was later to become his wife, Claire, in a manner that Hollywood directors would have loved to have captured. He took a lot of stick from the rest of us and now has the effrontery to deny it was him. Looking at the description above, none of us could have got it wrong.

His career and mine crossed many times. I am pleased to say as he worked with me at Eurotunnel as well as in several positions on the railway, where we would regularly meet.

During an exercise at Derby when we practised a derailment situation through role play, Mike and David Cruttenden were the driver and second man of a freight train that was involved. Somehow they got hold of cloth caps to bring authenticity and decided they would test out John Powell, who was playing the area manager, by seeing if they could purloin some of the cigarettes that had spilled during the 'accident'. John was equal to his task and David and Mike were nearly eaten by a police dog which was guarding the spoils.

Mike did not believe in indecision. He was a natural operator who relied on his 'gut feeling' and experience. You never went short of a plan and events moved swiftly when Mike was in charge. He possessed a natural enthusiasm for the job, seemingly so lacking these days, and he expected his colleagues to be the same.

We played Turkey in the game Diplomacy while on a course at Derby, and he has never forgiven me for losing the whole game through being tricked by Trevor Halversen, who eventually became the European Manager for British Rail, a highly political job - there must be a message there somewhere.

I remember Mike particularly for the interest he showed. He was always keen to know how things were and if there was ever any question of a problem he would always be willing to try and help sort it. He has retired now, and typically is seriously considering doing VSO in order to 'put something back'. He was always generous with his skills and talent. I know he will do a wonderful job if he does go.

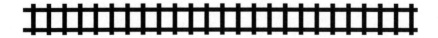

CHAPTER 4

STRATFORD AND LIVERPOOL STREET

In between spells of working at Temple Mills I alternated with positions at Stratford and in the control organisation at Liverpool Street. I was Assistant Station Manager, then Station Manager at Stratford between 1971 and 1975, where I began to learn my trade in the passenger railway. There were areas/station managers at Liverpool Street, Stratford, Ilford, Shenfield (latterly), Chelmsford, Colchester and Southend Victoria.

The Stratford area was small geographically, taking only Bow Junction and Stratford signal boxes on the main line and down to North Woolwich on the line through Canning Town and Custom House. There were freight yards at Mile End, Bow Midland, Stratford Market, Plaistow, Silvertown, Thames Wharf and Old Ford and the huge carriage sidings at Thornton's Field - often wrongly spelt Thorntons Fields.

My particular responsibility was the North Woolwich line, with Bob Cousins managing the other freight yards and Harry Faulkner looking after all things commercial for the area. Jack Caley was my Station Manager when I was an assistant station manager, and I could not have asked for a better and more experienced teacher.

My responsibilities included, in particular, visiting the various signal boxes along the route. There were boxes at Fork Junction, just below the main line at Stratford, where the diesel trains would be turned from Stratford low level; Stratford Southern at the country end of the down platform at Stratford low level; Abbey

Gates, controlling the exit/entry to Stratford Market; Abbey Mills, just London side of Canning Town and controlling a piece of four-track railway; Thames Wharf between Canning Town and Custom House, controlling the yard at Thames Wharf also, and Custom House, controlling the entry to the two single lines, passenger and freight, to North Woolwich and Silvertown Yard respectively.

Visits to signal boxes involved a relatively strict process, in that it was necessary to sign the train register book in which all the train movements and times were recorded and generally observe that the process of signalling was being carried out properly and according to the rules. The whole principle of signalling, even now, relies on 'one train in one section at one time'. 'Two trains in one section' to this day sends a shiver through an operator's spine.

All the boxes were operated by lever frames and block instruments. The single lines from Custom House were controlled by a token and the procedure was referred to as 'one engine in steam'. It became 'one train working' - perhaps 'one diesel in oil' would have been better at the time!

The boxes were worked mostly by young aspiring signalmen, eg Tommy Sparling at Abbey Mills, who graduated to Bow Junction, but there were one or two old timers. Fred at Thames Wharf had been there seemingly since Adam was a lad and was very experienced. On my first visit there, I noticed with a mixture of trepidation and elation that there was a portable radio on the box table. Trepidation because I would have to act, as radios were forbidden, and elation because I could show Fred I knew the rules and could not be treated in such a cavalier fashion.

'Fred' I said, 'you know better than that. What's this doing here?'

'Oh that' said Fred. 'It doesn't work'. I let it be known that I had not just fallen out of a Christmas tree, but Fred enjoined me to open the back of it. There was nothing inside; it was just an empty box, nothing that would make a radio work at all. It turned out Fred repaired radios and since the signal box was quiet in the extreme I could see nothing wrong with that. I withdrew, chastened.

Another hobby was practised at Custom House. The signalman there was a painter of extraordinary ability. At my suggestion, he submitted his work to the Royal Academy and was accepted. The other shift was worked, unusually, by a woman. As a result the box was like a new pin, all the brass polished, all taps gleaming and the floor like a mirror. The only leveller was that whoever entered the box had, as in a mosque, to remove their shoes. It was difficult to administer any from of discipline with no shoes on. Maybe that is part of the reason why shoes are removed on entering a mosque - no arguments with the Imam!

While passenger traffic on the branch was sporadic at best, mainly due to the infrequent service, there was a small amount of activity around the freight yards. Stratford Market acted as a secondary yard and sorted the few wagons that still delivered produce to the market, the odd bogie bolster wagons (long-wheelbase wagons for carrying steel) for the Sanders and Fosters siding located on the upside of the up electric/single line between Stratford and Bow Junction (now the Docklands Railway), any traffic for Thames Wharf, and coal for Plaistow and West Ham yard located between Canning Town and Custom House. Trains for Silvertown were run direct from Temple Mills. Silvertown also had a small secondary yard and sorted wagons for Tate & Lyle sugar and the Silvertown Tramway, which was in its declining years. The tramway had been constructed to serve the factories that had sprung up on the river frontage with the advent of the London Docks. It can still be traced, as it is now a walkway.

Towards the end of my time at Stratford, the Tate & Lyle traffic passed in hopper wagons as a trainload. They were loaded by a hopper in the yard. While I was watching the operation one day, the Tate & Lyle foreman came over.

'Still untouched by human hand' he said proudly. He drew the skirt of the hopper aside to reveal the sugar pouring into the wagon. He put his hand in and withdrew a fist full of sugar. 'Yes, untouched by human hand' he said. Before I could stop him, to my horror he drew the skirt aside again and threw the sugar back into the wagon.

* * * * *

One of the more arcane procedures in coal yards was the measuring of excess space. Coal merchants, as part of their agreement, rented a set square footage, and were notorious for using more than their allotted and paid-for area. In order to combat this and to provide a disincentive, the Divisional Office would include a date on their circular to all areas when it would be necessary to visit the yards and measure the space currently in use by each merchant.

Armed with a tape measure, I would turn up on the allotted day at Plaistow looking very official. The conversation would go something like this.

Coal Merchant: I don't believe it.

RJM: Believe what?

Coal Merchant: Did you pass a lorry on the way in? It's just this second left. He's just dropped all this coal here, way over my area. I asked him not to, but... I've got my shovel here ready to move it and lo and behold you turn up to measure excess space.

RJM: (not looking quite so official now) That puts me in a difficult position.

Coal Merchant: Let's have a cuppa - come in. Bloody hell, just remembered, got given a bottle of malt the other day - can't abide the stuff - would you like it?'

At this point, tape measures would be rolled back up and put back into official-looking briefcases. Tea would be drunk, the bottle of malt would join the tape measures and a nil return submitted to the Divisional Office. I must stress this did not happen often, but happen it certainly did.

Stratford Market was ruled by Norman Jolly, the supervisor. He was a very affable and personable man, as was Dick Jones, the other supervisor, but he transformed like Jekyll into Hyde if you tried to suggest some saving could be made on either hours or numbers. There were two shunters on each of the two shifts and a number taker. To cover the 'busy period' a pilot engine was also allocated. Therefore, to deal with probably eight wagons per day, there were 11 staff without any relief. It is to my eternal discredit that I did not bite the bullet and do something about it, but an easy life seemed more attractive. I do not believe the inaction brought about the Market's downfall, as it would have shut anyway. Now the Jubilee Line depot hides the evidence.

Silvertown yard was supervised by Charlie Auger, a railwayman of long standing. The yard was allocated a pilot engine and a couple of shunters. The yard was open only for one shift however, and was far more productive than the market because of Tate & Lyle.

Because of its neighbourhood there were several scrap yards around the railway; one was located at the edge of Canning Town down platform. We received several complaints that the scrap was spilling over, sometimes on to the platform itself, clearly a dangerous event. I decided to take the law into my own hands and visit the offices of the group concerned. I noticed a green Rolls Royce outside and felt an air of apprehension on entering the office.

'Who's in charge?' I barked. After a period of silence, a very smartly dressed man appeared. He had a handkerchief in his top pocket, silk shirt and silk matching tie. He was thick set and exuded a menacing demeanour

'I'm in charge' he said, in an authoritative tone 'What do you want?'

'I'll tell you what I want!' I said fiercely, 'I want you to stop your scrap getting on my platform; otherwise someone is going to be killed'.

The smart man eyed me for a moment, and it seemed the office held its collective breath.

'I like your cheek, son' he said. 'It will be done.'

With that he left the office. Staff slid out from behind desks and filing cabinets. I was informed in hushed tones that I had just met one of the Kray twins. Interestingly, the scrap was cleared away, and no more encroached on to the platform.

* * * * *

Part of the Assistant Station Manager's duties involved overseeing the main line operations, particularly in the peak, between Bow and Maryland inclusive. It was usual to do this from the main Stratford signal box, which was until very recently on the London end of Platform 10 overlooking the station. It was fringed by Forest Gate towards Shenfield and Bow Junction towards London. The panel was divided into A, B and C panels with A and B being responsible for the Main and Cambridge lines and C for the area around High Meads.

A and B panels were good to work. The route indications were demonstrated mechanically by the panel itself, which had on it a representation of the points outside that moved mechanically, ie routes set were not shown by lights, as in C panel, but by white sections being exposed against the green panel. The route set therefore showed up in white.

Alec Fyffe, one of the best signalmen there, nearly gave me

heart failure when he pointed out an apparent run through at high speed. (This would mean that a train had passed over a set of points that were set the wrong way.) Actually the points on the ground were fine, but the point indicators on the panel had 'stuck' the wrong way.

It was an excellent atmosphere, but when the service went wrong it was hard work, as we had to be very sure we had sent trains to Liverpool Street on the correct inbound line. A mistake could ruin the evening peak in particular. Bow Junction was the last opportunity to transfer trains from the main to electric line or vice versa, or to try and reverse the positions of trains. Such processes could be vital in achieving the correct platforming sequences at Liverpool Street.

There were two signalmen, who carried out the same functions in completely opposite ways. Charlie Wade would throw the door to the box open and arrive with much noise and fanfare. He would set a route by turning the switch on the signalling panel at the route commencement and banging the exit button with his fist. Everything was done at great speed and with much ceremony.

Colin however slid on duty and seemed to appear from nowhere. He had a habit of turning the entry switch and pausing momentarily before gently pushing the exit button. That moment's pause was for thought - have I got this right? Both were good signalmen, and to my knowledge both had an unblemished record, but they were so different in style.

George Vincent, a member of the illegal Union of Railway Signalmen (URS), did not immediately take to me. He asked me fairly early on why I went to the box for the peak.

'To make sure you do what you should' I said.

'You wouldn't know if we did or didn't' he retorted.

I made a bargain with him. He was to get the tea and I would signal the morning peak. He didn't know I had been taught well by Alec Fyffe. Once I had proved my worth, we became good friends. Since George was a tall man he even coveted my trousers when I had finished with them - he always made out he could not afford to buy new ones.

My limited knowledge of signalling came in very handy on one unfortunate occasion. I had been told of a signalman drinking on duty at Bow Junction. Signalmen will not shy away from reporting this sort of behaviour, and I therefore decided to go with Paul Nowak, the ASM, and pay the box a visit at about 19.00. No signalman was to be found on duty. He had left the box in the charge of the box lad, who normally just recorded the details of train running. He was no more than 17.

I left Paul in the box and went to the nearest pub. There was the signalman, downing a pint as I walked through the door. Sadly, both the signalman and the lad were sent home and it was now down to me to work the box. I let the signalmen both sides, Stratford and Bethnal Green, know what was going on and settled down to put the knowledge that Alec Fyffe had given me to good use. The route setting was OK, but I had reckoned without the tannoy system from Thornton's Field Carriage Sidings opposite.

At the London End, the outlet of the carriage sidings, was a cabin in which worked the 'pointsman'. His job was to set the roads inside the depot in that area and to tell the signalman at Bow where trains were going that were leaving the yard.

After about an hour of working the box the speaker crackled. 'Engtoshffedal' came the call. Paul and I reckoned this could be translated as 'engine to shed', so I pulled off, and after the locomotive had exited the yard set the road for the carriage line to take it towards Stratford shed.

The driver came on the signal post telephone. 'I'm supposed to go back on B road into the carriage sidings' he said. 'My fault' I replied. 'Wait your signal.' I cancelled the route, and after the two minutes' backlock pulled off the correct route. (Whenever a route is set on the railway and it is cancelled without any train passing over it, there is a backlock of two minutes for safety reasons.)

All was well. All that is except for Harry Cornish, the pointsman. The tannoy sprang into life again. This time I could understand. 'Effin' signalmen', he pronounced, 'seventy quid a week and you can't understand English!'

'Sorry Harry, my fault' I said.

'Your fault! I should think it was' he said, and for the rest of the time I was in the box Harry chuntered on about it. I had forgotten to tell him it was me working the box, and he had no idea he was whittling on to his station manager.

Somebody must have told him later however, for at 09.00 the next morning there was a knock on my office door and in came Harry. I have never, before or since, seen anyone take his cap off by sliding it down his head, never leaving contact with his skin. 'Governor' he said, 'I wanted to apologise...'

'Sit down Harry' I interrupted, looking as stern as possible. We parted on good terms and all was smoothed over.

* * * * *

There was a relatively large admin office dealing with the station rosters, banking, staff records etc. And then there was Nell. Nell was about 4' 9" tall, but she wore a hair piece that made her about 5' 6". She made the tea and ran messages. Between the hours of 08.00 and 12.00 she would produce roughly 12 cups of tea. Passengers who waited around Platform 10 would have been forgiven if they wondered at the regular procession of managers visiting the toilets.

I decided one day to take the matter into my own hands and carefully poured the 11th tea into a plant. I experienced that terrible feeling that I was being watched, turned and saw Nell observing the dreadful deed. I don't think she ever forgave me.

One payday, we were raided. As with so many events like that, a meeting was held long after the horse had bolted to see what we could do to tighten up security. After the great and good had left, Jack Caley remarked that it was all a waste of time. He painted a scene where gunmen shouted though a locked door that they had the Station Manager outside with a gun to his head. We were to open up or they would blow his head off. 'What would you do?' asked Jack. He was not impressed with the unanimity of opinion that the Area Manager and Charles I might have something in common.

The day-to-day station activity was overseen by three supervisors, Len Ramsden, Bert Davies and Jack Ward, who were located on Platform 9/10 underneath the box. The character of the group was Jack Ward, who had seen many years' service and had a wicked sense of humour.

While I was there as an ASM, I bought my first house at Chelmsford for the princely sum of £6,500. I was, therefore, the proud owner of my first garden, and I much enjoyed both the planning and the graft that was associated with it.

Jack came to my office one day and gave me a package of plants, individually wrapped in damp blotting paper. 'Plant these out' he said. 'About one foot apart. Make sure they get manure or dried plant food regularly.'

I carefully chose the spot and lovingly planted each one. My parents came to visit for the first time and to my horror, having left my mother in the garden on her own, I went out to find my cosseted blooms lying in a tangled heap on the path.

'What are you doing?' I exclaimed.

'Weeding' she said.

I had been well and truly 'had' by Jack. At that moment I turned revenge into an art form. I let Jack know that I enjoyed the joke and we all guffawed as necessary.

Jack was a lover of pickled onions, and when I noticed he was down to his last one I obtained a clove and inserted it into the middle of the onion. On visiting his office I asked if I could have the onion, even if it was his last one. I knew he would refuse and indeed he immediately popped it into his mouth and bit hard. The resultant combination takes some imagination, and mine does not stretch that far. As I left the office I again thanked Jack, who was still puce and choking, for the 'weeds'. Revenge was sweet, or in this case, bitter.

I experienced my first suicide at Stratford. A man jumped from the platform at Maryland on to the up main line in front of an express from Norwich travelling almost at full speed. Jack Caley took the call, and knowing I had not seen such things, he asked me to go with him. I was affected more, as I always have been since - about 12 times - by the waste of a life rather than the resultant mess. That has always been a nuisance more than anything else, stopping us from running the railway.

I remember when a woman got off a train arriving at the Down Electric platform expressed an interest in what was going on, I suggested it might be better not to look. She did not heed my advice and looked on to the Up Main to see Jack carrying a piece of the unfortunate gentleman up the track. The ticket collector said he did not see her leave the station but felt a whoosh of wind as she flew by.

The other issue after such an event was getting your appetite back. Not for Jack. When we arrived back at Stratford he disappeared into his office for a moment and emerged eating a ham sandwich.

* * * * *

It was notoriously difficult to organise simple work or repairs on and around the station. To have a window repaired, for instance, a works order had to be completed with a priority rating on it and submitted in triplicate to the engineer's offices at Stratford. They would allocate someone to carry out the work eventually, usually when the people who had requested the repair had long since contracted frostbite.

This was where the value of a man like Spider became evident. Spider, or to give him his proper name Fred Robinson, had been given the sobriquet back in the mists of time, and the reasons for it were long lost. He carried out all minor and some major works and was viewed askance by the engineers, who saw him as purloining their work. It was not only their work that Spider stole. A can of paint, carelessly put down and ignored for seconds, would disappear effortlessly, while a hammer and chisel, left alone for a moment, would apparently walk off into thin air. Every piece of wood, pot of paint, hinge or any piece of equipment Spider used had once been the property of the Engineering Department Stratford.

Spider needed to work somewhere, and his workshop was located in the subway from the old entrance to the station to Platforms 9/10. No one was allowed in there until I finally insisted I should be permitted to view the premises. It was an Aladdin's cave of tools, wood, metal, paint etc. Worse than that, Spider had tapped into the main gas, electric and water supplies for the station to provide creature comforts. When I write 'tapped' into, I mean sawn into. How a fire was not started when he cut the gas pipe remains a mystery.

Only very recently, Spider's workshop was uncovered during refurbishment for the Olympics. No one knew its history until I was able to furnish the details. In these days of intensive budget scrutiny with a less romantic and perhaps less practical slant to it, we would never have got away with Spider. He saved us a fortune however, and constituted one of those characters for whom the railway was rightly famous.

I conducted many interviews of job applicants. Two stick in my mind.

The form to apply for a job was comprehensive, as one would expect. One of the sections was concerned with the applicant's health, and one completed form caught my eye; it told me the applicant was 12 feet tall. It was with some interest that I awaited his arrival, but I was disappointed to find that my hopes of putting him forward to Bertram Mills' circus were dashed on his entry. He was tall, but not 12 feet. I asked him how he had come to fill in the form in this way. He removed his shoe and showed me the sole. On it was imprinted the figure 12, indicating the size of the shoe, but he had read the 'feet' box under size as shoe size.

Another applicant had put on his form that he had attended a mental hospital for two years. In those more enlightened days it was possible to ask questions at an interview that really mattered. Now an interviewer would be seen as discriminatory if this point was discussed but I asked him if he would tell me what had happened and whether he had fully recovered. He did better than that. He produced a piece of paper.

'There's my certificate of sanity' he said. 'Where's yours?' Collapse of stout party.

* * * * *

When the Stratford area expanded we took responsibility for Poplar Dock. The dock, close to the old London Group, was reached by a track that led from Victoria Park signal box, where a train from Temple Mills would 'run round' (transfer the locomotive from one end of the train to the other), since there was no facing lead from the line towards Camden Road direct to the dock. The line, running south, passed under the GE main line near Bow Junction and down to Poplar. The Docklands Railway now occupies the track bed through Devons Road and Bow Church.

The dock was originally owned by Great Western Railway, providing them with a strategic outlet in London. The main traffic was steel, wood and copper bars, and most of the first two was imported from Russia, with Africa providing the copper. The Russian boats were skippered by men who could have come straight from the pages of the David Lowe cartoon books. Huge, sweatered, sweating, bearded bears of men would emerge from the bridge, spy me on the quayside and roar for me to join them. Usually a fatal error, since some hours later and some pints of 'wodka' later, I would stagger down the gangplank like an animal awakening from the vet's tranquilliser.

Sometimes a play was enacted with the trade unions. I would arrive to find nothing was happening on the quayside. I would sit in my office and wait. Within about five minutes there would be a knock on my door and the local convener would come in. Pleasantries would be exchanged. Then: 'Governor, we've got a boat in from Russia - God knows how they loaded it, the steel beams are too long and unless we pick the boat up we can't get them out'. With all the solemnity of a consultant being called to a patient with heart failure, I would proceed to the quayside and peer into the ship's hold.

'What about job and knock?' I would say [another phrase for job and finish-one job then go home.]Within about an hour the boat would be unloaded and the quayside returned to its quiet inactive state, since they had all gone about their other businesses.

The police reported to me one day that they had good reason

to believe that copper ingots on their way to Eastleigh were being stolen from hi-fit wagons loaded from the boats. The wagons were shunted into the 'field' sidings ready for a locomotive to attach and take them on to Eastleigh, where they were made mostly into copper wire. I joined the police in the admin offices about 16.00 and we watched.

Sure enough, a gang of platelayers arrived, unloaded two ingots on to the grass beside the sidings and started to bury them, with the obvious intention of picking them up later in a lorry. Within seconds the scene had turned into an episode from the Sweeney, complete with Jack Regan shouting 'You're nicked!' The arrested were led away in a very sorry chain gang.

It remained to move the evidence back to the waiting police cars, and these ingots were very heavy. I offered to drive the Drury locomotive, the Poplar shunting locomotive, to pick them up. I knew how to engage the gear by lifting a trap in the floor, but I could not budge the loco despite revving the engine so much that it nearly disintegrated. In desperation I telephoned Frank Heslop, Area Manager and engineer. He arrived by car, got on to the footplate and looked at my handiwork.

'Always remember, a locomotive will move far more easily if the handbrake is not applied' he said quietly. It took me a long time to live that one down.

Poplar was an experience in the same category as Temple Mills. Both operations have disappeared from the transport scene in this country and I count myself as lucky to have been a part of managing these fascinating and challenging places.

By that time the area had grown and was under the leadership of Frank Heslop, who had previously been Depot Manager at Stratford. The depot and the footplate staff were now included and there must have been well over 1000 staff working in the area.

Frank was a delightful, laid-back Yorkshire man. It was rumoured that he had once got off a train at Doncaster and his shoes had gone on to York, which if you knew Frank was a real possibility. Frank was an engineer and understood virtually nothing of operations. I saw it as a crusade and a challenge for me to get him to come out on the area and visit a signal box or a yard.

Eventually I ushered him into Temple Mills East signal box. I introduced him to the signalman and Frank spent some minutes studying the panel in silence, hands in pockets, stomach slightly thrust forward in typical Heslopian fashion.

'Well,' he said eventually, 'tell me what all these lights mean.' I wished I hadn't bothered!

As I have said, I moved between Stratford and Liverpool Street as I climbed up the management grades. I was appointed to two positions, both in charge of the control office and one more senior than the other - they were named 'operating assistants'. I worked with Mike Jones and Chris Daughton at first, under Peter Martin, who was the senior assistant. Mike would often state that he had taken a decision and that since he was the 'senior man' the decision was final. That label has stuck down the years and he is still referred to as the senior man.

Our job was closely concerned with the day-to-day running of the division's operational railway through the control office. We were on call and this, in the days before mobile phones, was a problem. Each time you changed location you had to contact the control and tell them the new contact number. Mobile phones would have been useful on site, as often the nearest telephone would be in the nearest signal box, which could be a good walk away. On site therefore you felt very much as those naval commanders must have felt in Tudor and Elizabethan times, taking decisions that their bosses could well disagree with and result in criticism.

Every morning a conference would be held internally within the division to review the previous day and what was happening currently. Following this a conference was held with York control. Norwich, King's Cross attended this meeting with us, and regardless of what chaos might be unfolding in our patch we always told York everything was fine. The Norwich representative would lead off in that delightful accent about the 06.20 from Norwich being five minutes late etc. We would say nothing. Better not to get involved - we always believed that no one else understood our railway.

The function of the control office was to ensure that the railway performed in line with the service offer, or timetable. All the information necessary to achieve this was stored in the office; all the crew diagrams or work schedules, all the working timetable information on train running, all emergency contact numbers and constant liaison with the electrical controllers who were responsible for the control of the 25kv overhead line.

When everything was running normally it would be fair to say that there wasn't so much to do. There were always problems of regulation, particularly freight trains, and usually there was a crew off-diagram that had to be dealt with. However, when problems arose, the control came into its own. It would manage any service changes and would determine strategy. Will the railway be stopped for a time to try and clear a problem? Would single-line working be instituted? Would diversions be made, and what would happen to passengers who were 'stranded'? What buses were required? The control would be looking forward to see how the incident could be cleared up and when normal services could be resumed.

The worst problem was that of train crew. Once crew were displaced from their schedule, it was not only difficult to keep track of them but to plan who would cover the working that they should have been doing. I always thought the train crew controller had the worst job. Units can't complain - train crew certainly can!

The slotting in of freight trains in a predominantly passenger division was difficult, and fell to the assistant deputy chief controller and the controller on table 6 that managed the area around Temple Mills.

Hoaxes have often been played on people on their last day at work, but I have never seen one as elaborate as the situation that was set up for Stan Moore on his last day on the railway. He was a controller on the table that covered the line to Cambridge, Ely and Kings Lynn, taking over from the table that looked after Bethnal Green and Liverpool Street. On his last shift, late turn, Bob Smith and others had devised a fictitious freight train that left Tottenham coal depot at 17.40, right in front of the 17.36 Liverpool Street to King's Lynn. It was a class 9 - ie maximum speed 25 mph. Freight trains were completely forbidden during the peak at the best of times, but it was unheard of for a Class 9 in particular to be allowed anywhere near those busy hours.

Not only had the others invented this train, they had also calculated all the delays that would ensue and provided all the details to all the signalmen down the line. Stan therefore received the information about the errant train and then received more information throughout the next two hours that showed a picture of mayhem out on the ground. I think the Lynn was showing 80 minutes late by Cambridge. Everything else suffered as well, and Stan was in a state of complete shock by 20.00 when we let him out of his misery. Outside, the peak had worked like clockwork, controlled by Bob Smith. I cannot report Stan's comments when he was told of the trick.

* * * * *

The deputy chief controllers in the office - the shift managers

- were legends in their own right. Alf Linsted, who always called me 'son'; the lovely Ben Firman, who was one of the most gentle people I have ever met and extremely proficient; Allan Clarke, who was professional in the extreme; and Bob Mace, whose ability to imitate celebrities immediately endeared me to him. His Richie Benaud could have fooled the Australian cricket team.

We took it in turns to cover the morning and evening peaks. On my first week of on call, a Colchester driver passed BG8 signal on the down main at danger just leaving Liverpool Street and ploughed through the side of a Chingford train crossing on to the up suburban line. To my relief, Peter Martin went to the site and I was left to run what we could of the service.

On another occasion Alec Fyffe rang me from Bethnal Green early in the morning to tell me the system was allowing him to set conflicting routes (ie set up a crash). We stopped working immediately and discovered that an error had been made in the signalling wiring at the end of a possession - a frightening occurrence.

The control office ran on paper and telephones. Each running controller was connected to the signal boxes in his area, accessing them through an individual switch that was a line direct to each box. By depressing the switch the controller alerted the signalman and vice versa. We would ring each box fairly regularly for a 'square up' and be told the passing times of each train. On the sheet on the desk was each service, separated into up and down, with the booked passing time against each signal box. The entry would either be ticked (on time) circled (early) or the number of minutes late written against the train concerned. The phrase was therefore, 'Are we all ticks and rings this morning?'

When on call I was called out to many incidents. Two stick in my mind. The first was at Tilbury, and I recall it because I was proud of my diagnosis of the reason for the derailment. A parcels train was propelling (being pushed by the locomotive) into Tilbury Riverside station (no longer there) and when I arrived on site the leading pair of wheels was derailed, having taken the incorrect route. But the points lay in the correct direction and the rest of the train had taken the right route. The guard who was in charge at the leading end of the propelling move said that the dolly or subsidiary signal had cleared and yet the points had moved under the train. The signalman confirmed he had set the route and pulled the signal off.

What had happened was that the guard had just anticipated the signal coming off and called his train back. As the train started to move, the signalman called for the route. The leading wheels were just on the points and effectively locked them. As soon as the leading wheels had passed over the points, the motor operated and the points went into the reverse position, thus allowing the rest of the train to go right route.

The second incident involved a JCB digger. Some vandals had succeeded in starting one parked near the railway just Clacton side of Colchester at about 00.30 and managed to steer it down the bank so that the shovel had embedded itself into the four-foot. The line was blocked and needed to be clear for the morning peak, the first train off Clacton being about 05.40. I arrived on site at the same time as the digger driver, who had been called out. He couldn't start the machine and I asked for the crane from Colchester. However, when the crane arrived on site it was clear we could not lift the digger easily because there were fuel pipes running down the sides which were very vulnerable.

Mr Calvert, the Divisional Operating Manager, was on the phone constantly to the signalman, saying he would not forgive me if I didn't clear the line for the morning peak. At about 05.30 I asked the driver to try and start the machine again. No luck, it would not start. The driver got out and kicked his machine in frustration. 'Try it now,' I said. Instant ignition, and the offending machine was driven off the railway just in time for the morning peak to begin on time.

One of the most difficult processes to carry out well in disruption is dissemination of information. It is probably the most frequent complaint from our customers that no one told them what was going on, and similarly our staff also were not well informed. In the days before computers, email and all the social media that now exist, in the event of the control office needing to send out a revised timetable, perhaps for an evening peak, there was little alternative other than to ring each station and tell them what was taking place. Telex machines were seen as the answer, and Chris Daughton and I decided to purchase machines for each station on the division. I rang a supplier based in Brighton. The interest from the receptionist was fairly cursory until I mentioned the figure of 290 machines. I found myself talking to the MD within seconds, and he invited Chris and me to his offices for a demonstration.

On arrival we were ushered into a room populated by machines and a very impressive Chief Sales Manager, who told us he was Rear Admiral, RN retired. In a typical plummy accent he told Chris and me to stand by a machine and announced he would send a message from the other side of the room, which would instantaneously appear on our machine.

He tapped in the message. All remained silent and inactive. 'Is it there yet?' he asked. We peered at the machine closely. 'Nothing yet' we answered. He tapped again. Still nothing. In a fluster he telephoned someone called Joe and asked him to come in.

Joe wore a brown coat, cloth cap and had the obligatory roll up protruding from his mouth. Our Rear Admiral explained the situation - how important we were etc - and Jo remained unimpressed. He peered over the back of our machine, removed his roll up and said 'I should turn the bloody thing on if I were you'. With that he left. Comment from the Rear Admiral, which is ingrained on my mind: 'One must have such a man!'

During the 1970s there were several 'work to rules' staged by ASLEF at some of the depots in the division, especially Southend. On such occasions we were rostered around the clock to be ready for any eventuality. Eventually it was decided to put the management foot down and we would be instructed under certain circumstances to send home a driver who would not abide by the normal working rules. Gradually a resolution would be reached and the protest would end.

On nights there was not much going on. To my eternal shame, one evening several of the control and I set out for London and Soho in particular. We went into a particularly seedy club where the seats were arranged cinema style. The distorted music stopped and the lights went down. Over the loudspeaker came the announcement. 'And now, the lovely Lolita'. The lights went up, the music agonised itself to a start and the curtains opened. Nothing happened. No sign of anyone. The music stopped, the lights went out and the curtains closed. The same ritual was enacted two or three times until, over the loudspeaker, came the frustrated question 'where the effing 'ell is Lolita?'

A little later in the show one of the young ladies came off the stage and sat on the lap of a customer in the front row. To our amazement he was a very senior manager from the division. When we arrived back at the office I took the card that we had taken from the establishment and left it on his desk with a message saying 'We saw you'. There was quite a stir, as I understand it, but no enquiry. I wonder why?

The team of senior operational managers at Liverpool Street

worked well. Ray Unwin ('Daddy Long Legs') was passenger operations, Dick Ball the freight manager. Together with the operating assistants we were all overseen by Brian Driver, followed by Roy Calvert as Divisional Operating Manager. It was one episode in my career where a great feeling of teamwork existed. We were driven hard, especially by Roy, who would give no quarter and expected the highest of standards, but we were driven fairly. We worked hard and we played hard - an ideal balance.

My first association with the Stratford area finished in 1977, when I was appointed Area Manager Tinsley.

HARRY FAULKENER

Harry was the Assistant Station Manager at Stratford in 1972 when I went there as an ASM myself. My responsibility, together with Bob Cousins, was for operations and Harry looked after the 'commercial' side of the business, namely ticket office accounts and all the aspects of freight rates, including demurrage and standage.

Harry always dressed in the regulation uniform suit and exuded an air of authority tinged with benevolence and a somewhat avuncular approach. He was a very keen West Ham supporter. In fact that is an understatement - he was fanatical. Monday mornings could be either joyful or terrifying. There was never a need to look it up to know whether the Hammers had won or not, because Harry's behaviour gave the result away. The door from platform 11 would open and one of two things occurred. Either Harry would neatly slide his case across the polished floor with the precision of a champion bowler to bring it to rest alongside his desk, or throw it very hard across the office. You can guess which meant a win and which a defeat.

Harry practised another trick which I was never able to master. He could karate chop the receiver of the phone so that it sprang from its cradle and hovered in mid-air. He would deftly catch it and make or answer his call. I broke several phones trying the same thing until Jack Caley, the Area Manager, told me to desist.

Harry retired when I was Station Manager and it fell to me to make the presentation. Here was a man who had given a lifetime of service to the railway, most of it in East London; a man who had been scrupulously honest throughout his career and was well respected and liked; a man who had not risen to great heights but had done a sound and excellent job. Not easy to sum up in a presentation, but I hope I did him justice. He deserved it.

JOHN FORRESTER

Nobody is absolutely sure where Chief Divisional Signalling Inspectors come from. Everyone knows they are a race apart, and I always was in awe of them. Their knowledge was seemingly limitless, but their secret was that they could put it into practice and gain total respect, and not a little fear, from those around them. I worked closely with two such men and consider myself privileged to have met both of them.

When I went to Bristol to take up the position of Assistant Divisional Movement Manager, I met John Forrester, Chief Signalling Inspector of the Bristol Division. John had a delightful West Country drawl. He spoke slowly and deliberately and it was easy to underestimate his intelligence from his somewhat languid demeanour.

The first time I met him, he took me to Bristol Power Box. On arriving at the panel that signalled the Avonmouth branch, he said to the signalman, 'For your benefit and mine let's go through the special working arrangements that apply on this branch, particularly under failure conditions'. He proceeded, together with the signalman, to describe the processes. It wasn't for his benefit or for the signalman's - it was for mine. That was John's way.

I understand that when John became Regional Signalling Inspector for the Western Region, on his first visit to Old Oak Common signal box near Paddington, he was regarded on first impressions as I have described above - what can this dear old buffer up from the country tell us?

I understand that after about an hour John called the attention of the box and told them in no uncertain terms that this was not the way it would be run in future. He proceeded to let all know that he would expect far higher standards. On being challenged by some he completely destroyed them with his logic and knowledge. All this was apparently carried out in the same measured drawl, quietly and uncompromisingly.

His staff adored him, and the management at Bristol and later Swindon recognised his immense worth. He was a man at the top of his game. I am not sure he will ever be replaced.

DAVID FOULKES

Ten years older than me, ex-military police, a formidable fast bowler who had played in the Lancashire leagues, David was the admin manager at Tinsley. He must have had heart failure when he heard that a southerner with a degree in Classics, ex-public school and only 29 years old, was coming to be the Area Manager.

Not long after I arrived, the management team went out for lunch to celebrate Christmas. The pub had a snooker table and it was decided that David and I would take on challengers. With my second shot, and I was nervous, it must be said, I peered at the table, trying to look very professional. As I bent to take my carefully-considered shot, the cue flicked from my hand and caught the black. It sailed straight into the furthest pocket, costing us dear. David's face told it all. You could see him think 'I knew he would be useless, I just knew it.'

We became very firm friends. He was direct, forceful, fierce, imposing and very, very quick on the repartee. He got things done, or to use his own phrase, he pulled trees up.

David had a wicked sense of humour which I found very appealing, and he was excellent at making sure I was protected at all times. Though loyal to a fault to me, he didn't find his way on to everyone's Christmas card list. He kept me on my toes and I loved working with him as a result. He was one of the most vibrant personalities I have encountered.

GLADYS

When I joined the railway, my father gave me one piece of advice (among many) which was to prove very useful. He told me there were three individuals I should make sure I got to know well and to make sure, without sycophantic overtones, that I kept the right side of them. They were the tea lady, the messenger and the security guard on the door.

Gladys was the tea lady in the Area Manager's Office at Paddington. She had almost reached retirement age when I arrived, and indeed retired while I was there. She had a gentle, kind face which always smiled at me, though I understood she could be forceful, shall I say, in her dealings with those she did not like. She saved her worst wrath for the union members who purported to represent her. Gladys fulfilled two of the key roles in the office, for she was also the messenger. She had a shock of blonde/white hair, stood about 5' 5'' tall and was fairly full of figure.

With Gladys, tea seemed to materialise from nowhere at just the moment it was required. She was the equivalent of Radar in MASH, always one step ahead. Her maternal instincts were very strong and manifested themselves in the provision of lunch or elevenses if she thought I was looking a little peckish. Above all she had a very kind heart.

On Friday evenings (as described elsewhere) Sir Peter Parker, Chairman of British Rail, would arrive at Paddington at about 16.30 and complete some work before taking the train to Charlbury. Gladys had a sixth sense about his arrival time. Tea was always on the desk, piping hot, as he entered the station.

Eventually Gladys retired, and following the party we held in her honour I announced that I would be taking her and the various gifts home in the area car. I first had to persuade her that it was in order for me to use the car for such purposes, and eventually we set off.

On arrival she invited me in for tea, and as she was preparing the brew I noticed three boxes of chocolates on the mantelpiece. They all had labels which read 'To Gladys with love and thanks, Peter.'

'What are these?' I asked. 'Why aren't they opened?'

'I'm not opening them' she said. 'Those were Christmas presents from Sir Parker' (sic). 'They stay there.'

There was no more to be said.

KEITH GRAFTON

Colleagues have heard me say many times that every business must have a Grafton. Keith worked with me at Chiltern and was the keeper of my conscience on rules and regulations. His standards were of the highest. He would brook no lessening of our response to safety or operations and often, moustache bristling, would admonish me for even thinking along a certain line.

Keith is a perfectionist but a true professional also. He had been a driver for many years and had moved into the management grades to manage drivers. He had been a Trades Union representative and demonstrated a steely resolve when making his point.

Keith kept us all on the straight and narrow. He was another of those who work hard in the background, their contribution unrecognised. It is good for me to be able to recognise it now. Without professionals like Keith the railway would not operate as safely as it does.

He also paid me the ultimate compliment. On my leaving Crossrail (I had taken him there from Chiltern where we first met), he wrote on my leaving card, 'always the governor.' That always makes me shiver.

STUART GRIFFIN

Imagine a strong Somerset drawl, a personality that loves a joke and a laugh, an eternal optimist and a quicksilver operating brain and you would be imagining Stuart Griffin.

When I went to Chiltern as Operations Director, Stuart had been acting in the job and was faced with me, a usurper. There was absolutely no kickback, no hint of petulance and no sign of disloyalty. Stuart gave me 100%.

It was as a current operator that he made his biggest impression on me. Roy Calvert was the best operating strategist I worked with, while Dave Winder was in the top drawer of day to day operations, but Stuart was probably the best minute-by-minute operator. He was based at Banbury while I was at Marylebone. Within an instant of anything going wrong and while I was still musing on the problem, Stuart would be on the phone. 'At Marylebone, move that driver off 4 on to 2, split the unit on 3 and ask the spare man to work the front to Aylesbury. Get the driver off one to the rear half of three and work the last three coaches to the sidings.' The list of instructions was delivered in staccato fashion. I had a job to write it down, let alone act on it.

Stuart had a formidable ability to grasp a situation very quickly and devise a plan with astonishing speed. I have often listened to experts outlining the need for expert systems in computers to help plan the railway out of a crisis. No need for computers; ring Stuart. There is no one better I know. I so enjoyed working with him.

CHAPTER 5

TINSLEY

Roy Calvert had moved to Divisional Manager Sheffield, and one day in the spring of 1977 I received a call that there was a vacancy for an Area Manager at Tinsley and it might be an idea if I put in for it. I had not even considered it, as it was two grades above my present level and moving two grades was almost unheard of. Added to that, I was only 29 and a southerner.

However, I applied, was interviewed and in the summer was appointed to the job. I think Roy had had a battle with personnel and the then Division Operating Manager Harry Amos, who, lovely man as he was, I am sure did not take kindly to some young rake from the south taking over the senior area on the division. On my way up to Sheffield on the train, I made a pact with myself that I would never drink alcohol at lunchtime again. It must be one of my longest-running kept resolutions.

Tinsley yard was to the north of the Sheffield station complex. It was another huge marshalling yard, designed very much as a copy of Temple Mills, but with updated facilities and one very major difference - the Dowty retarder system. This system differed from all others in that it ran on oil pressure and ingeniously not only retarded wagons that were going too fast but impelled those that were going too slowly.

Alongside the track, down each road into the yard, there were hammers set like pistons into bores. The weight and speed of the wagons were calculated electronically and the hammer would either stay up as the wheel approached it and retard the speed by being pushed into the oil, thus producing resistance, or the piston would stay retracted until the wheel went over it and would come up behind to impel it and speed it up. Thus wagons were always humped at 3 mph and the spillage was virtually non-existent because there were no 'rough shunts'

The highlight of any visit to Tinsley was a ride to the secondary yard via the feed road. This was a quarter-mile siding which was fitted with impellers only, so wagons were taken down there with no locomotive attached.

The retarders made a clicking noise, which made it very easy to be aware when humping stopped. The other characteristic was the breaking of one of the many joints that carried the oil. A huge spout of oil would rise skywards, looking as if we were in the middle of Texas and about to become very rich.

Trunk trains brought the traffic in and it was sorted much as with Temple Mills. Trips were then run to the various locations around the yard and these were always prefaced with the letter T. The tannoy system in the yard often referred to T21 or T15. We received a complaint one day from a local living close to the yard that the staff seemed always to be consuming large quantities of tea!

Tinsley had a unique position among railway facilities, as it was the only one Dr Beeching opened. A plaque proudly proclaimed this on the walls of the administration building. The words hid the truth of what happened on that day. Had the Romans been involved, they would have considered the auguries unfavourable. There was a file in my office which detailed, literally to the half second, where the great and good doctor would go and whom he would meet. One entry read, '13.53 proceed to hump top to observe wagons being shunted'. Unfortunately the first wagon derailed and

Dr B was treated not to a display of shunting but of re-railing by the Tinsley crane. Not a good start!

* * * * *

On my arrival at the Divisional Offices, Sheaf House, I talked with Harry Amos for a while and he then took me down to meet the team at Tinsley itself. It has always been a habit of mine to try and find something on the first day that will set the tone for the job. This was presented to me on a plate. As I entered the office, I noticed a red and green light on a plate bolted into the concrete wall alongside the door. After the pleasantries, I announced that I would like to take a walk around the yard with the Operating Manager, David Phillips. Before leaving I asked what the significance of the lights was.

'Brilliant system, chief,' said David Foulkes, the man in charge of all things administrative. 'When someone knocks on your door, you press green on the switch under the desk if you want the guy to come in or red if you want him to stay outside'.

'I'm running an office here,' I said quietly, 'not a bloody signal box. Get rid of it before I get back.' Despite David's remonstrations I would not be moved and set off on my first tour of the yard. I was told afterwards that the bolts were stuck fast and when they saw me returning to the office David took the law into his own hands and smashed the panel out with a massive hammer. It left a huge hole in the wall which I saw when I returned, but I said nothing.

The removal of the lights made me a hero overnight. Nobody liked them, for good reason, and everyone knew me as the new guy who had removed the signalling from his office. It certainly did me no harm.

There were about 1300 staff in the Tinsley area, which covered

Rotherham, though it was entirely freight. The main traffic was scrap for the four large works, Deepcar, Ickles and two at Tinsley Park, with a freight terminal at Sheffield, SFT. I learned very quickly that there were different grades of scrap and that what would do for one works would not do for another.

I learned too the perils of standage and demurrage. The former was a calculation based on how many wagons had gone into a works in a week and how many had come out. The difference, if unfavourable, amounted to the number of excess wagons times the rate per week, and this was the amount owed on standage. Demurrage was based on individual wagons, actual time spent in the sidings over three days and payment cut in. The system was hated by all the customers and in order to reach agreement the bills were renegotiated over lunch –usually to the detriment of the railway.

* * * * *

I lodged in the Rutland Arms until I moved the family to the area. It was a pub very close to the station and managed by Charles and Gladys. Charles always wore a suit, which looked slightly incongruous in the area where the pub was situated. Gladys was in charge, but as often is the case with a fierce lady, on the inside she had a heart of gold and could not have been kinder to me.

One of the breweries had provided the pub with an early Calendar Girls idea. January saw the model fully clothed and each month she removed an item of clothing. I can remember that on the night of November 30th a special licence was applied for and at 23.59 the pub was full. At the appointed hour Charles solemnly turned to December, to the accompaniment of much cheering. I really cannot recall if it was all worth it, but it certainly enhanced the takings that night.

I discovered very quickly that life was more serious in the north. ASLEF certificates that proclaimed periods of membership of the union were handed over with much ceremony and were often accompanied by moist eyes. People were rightly proud to give and receive them.

A general knowledge quiz was held regularly at the British Rail Staff Association (BRSA). In the south such an event was there for a good night out; in the North no quarter was given or asked. I entered an area managers' team and we totally misjudged the mood. Pete Howells, Area Maintenance Engineer Tinsley, was the last of our team to answer in the first round. 'How many fences does a horse have to jump in the Grand National?' came the question. 'All of them' said Pete without any hesitation. We laughed uproariously, and we laughed alone. I was docked a point for asking if we could have a mark for sheer cheek.

I found also that people were far more honest. They spoke their mind, and small talk was not common. The first union meeting I chaired with ASLEF went something like this. ASLEF chairman: 'Item 1 agreed; item 2 agreed; item 3 we'll discuss; item 4 you must be bloody joking; item 5 agreed'. I was advised that there was absolutely no point in discussing item 4, as what the chairman had said was law.

The ASLEF tradition of Mutual Improvement Classes (MIC), was very strong in the Sheffield Division and among other northern divisions. Each week, in their own time, footplate men would meet to discuss the rules and the technical workings of the locomotives. They built the most beautiful models of valve gear etc which were works of art in themselves. They were used for instruction. Teams from each depot would be formed of four contestants and they would battle it out in difficult and challenging quizzes run by the locomotive inspectors.

The questions would be set by them and each member of each team would stand in turn and be asked these somewhat intricate points. The first answer was the only one accepted and at the end of an answer, the team member sat down. The chairman of the judges would confer with his two colleagues and then announce the mark. This would be out of a possible three marks, and a small slip would lose half a mark immediately. The chairman would announce the result, two marks or 'two and a half marks'. This would be written up against the team member's name and so on until each team had answered six rounds or so.

The competitions were well attended, and I am delighted to report that Tinsley won the cup for two of the three years I was there, which resulted in the team making their area manager very drunk, the second time in the only gay pub in Sheffield!

* * * * *

On a particularly sad note, one of our staff reported his son missing during some dreadful icy weather. He lived at Treeton, where there was a colliery. It was located at the end of the yard adjacent to the reception sidings. As soon as the news became known, the colliery and the yard stopped and all of us, as if we were under some unwritten and unspoken agreement, spent the day searching everywhere we could think of. Unfortunately the lad was found under the ice at some local ponds. The letter we all received from his father was particularly poignant. I wonder still if the same response would have happened in the south.

The starkest example of the difference in attitude was the Tinsley reunion. This was held annually and arranged by the trades unions. It was financed from the proceeds of one fruit machine in the mess room.

I was invited as Area Manager and asked to be at Sheffield City Hall at 17.00. My wife asked me what it would be like. I answered that I thought there would be about 50 people and it would be a drink until about seven and that would be it. We arrived just on 17.00 to find the LDC chairman, Lol Christian, panicking as to where we were. He hurried us into the room. There were not 50 people but 1600. It was not just a drink, it was a full dinner, followed by a cabaret organised by Taffy, a roster clerk from Tinsley who had experience in the clubs of Sheffield. The evening went on until 23.00 and my wife and I spent a wonderful time meeting as many as we could of the 'old boys', whose stories were incomparable. The only blight on the evening was a fiery and misplaced speech by Bill Ronksley, who was a Sheffield man and an official of ASLEF, slating the management and me in particular. Lol was profuse in his apologies and Bill was never asked again.

I experienced another difference at the next year's party. I had become worried that there was nothing to eat later on in the evening and suggested that we provide a buffet at about 21.00. Lol was against the idea, but I would not be shifted. When the moment came I saw where Lol's experience and intuition was better than mine. Taffy approached the microphone at 21.00 to announce the buffet at one end of the room. If anyone had been standing between the guests and the buffet they would have been trampled to death. The room rose as one and stampeded to the tables like wildebeest at a river crossing, each guest carrying a plastic bag. Whole plates of food were tipped into the bags and in about three minutes the whole lot had disappeared as surely as a field of corn is destroyed by locusts. We abandoned the buffet idea and after that I listened to Lol more closely.

* * * * *

There was, however, ample opportunity to manage in a different way too. Each Friday, the admin office would have fish and chips brought from a shop in Brinsworth about a mile away. On one occasion when it was my turn to buy the lunch, one of the ladies in the office asked me to buy some budgerigar seed. Needless to say I forgot.

If a misdemeanour was committed on the railway, the 'accused' was issued with a Form 1 which listed the charge. He/she was allowed three days to reply, either accepting the charge or requesting an interview/hearing. When that was held, a Form 2 was issued detailing the punishment.

I was issued with a Form 1 for 'forgetting to purchase budgerigar food' which had been requested, resulting in the death of said budgerigar from starvation. I decided to use it as a training exercise. I requested an interview with an advocate and invited anyone who wanted to come to attend, to understand the disciplinary machinery better. The room was packed with staff, the most interested and amused spectators and the ASLEF representatives. Frank Seeds, train crew manager, took the hearing and I was represented by David Foulkes.

The end result was that I was found guilty and the punishment was that I receive no privileges for three weeks. I thought that would be an end to it, but the punishment was carried out. I was not asked to partake in fish and chips for that time, so if I wanted any lunch on a Friday I had to buy it myself!

HSTs (High Speed Trains) were introduced to the north around this time, and operators had to understand the trains in case they failed on your patch. We attended a training familiarisation day at Neville Hill. The point that remains in my memory is the part that dealt with the various isolating cocks in the skirt of the train. The instructor told us that the main ones were in the compartments marked H and Q. 'You can easily remember that' he said. 'All the cocks are in HQ!'

Around this time the Class 56 diesel locomotive was introduced to Tinsley depot. In fact Tinsley was one of the first depots to work with them. The depot was adjacent to the parkway, a dual carriageway that ran from Sheffield. Lol Christian, while changing ends on the locomotive, went to answer the call of nature. When he returned, his locomotive had gone. The brakes had bled off, and being on a gradient, the locomotive had rolled towards the Parkway and deposited itself on the inside lane. A car driver travelling the other way reported it and was promptly arrested by the police for being drunk or hallucinating on drugs! Lol was never allowed to forget the incident. I would always allude to it when things were becoming a little heated in union meetings.

* * * * *

To celebrate the 100th anniversary of ASLEF and the fact that branch number one was in Sheffield, I decided to stage an open day at the yard. It was the one and only open day held at Tinsley, and was a huge success. I asked ASLEF and the NUR (now RMT) to nominate charities that would receive the money taken, and we raised just over £4000.

Open days in railway locations attract a variety of people; families who come to show their children the steam engines, old railwaymen who relive their past, families of those who work there who are interested in seeing what goes on. The customers will also include 'railway anoraks' who come to take photographs of their favourite locomotives, in particular if they are out of their normal locations. There are those who purloin pieces of 'railwayana'. At the end of the day we went to move the Deltic locomotive and found that someone had unscrewed and removed the traction control lever!

One of the great attractions of Tinsley was the hump-shunting locomotives. They were two 350s coupled together, but one was a slave to the other and was modified in shape. They were type 13s and there were only three, all based at Tinsley. People travelled a long way to see them.

Among the volunteers was the MIC team and I was concerned about their captain, Johnnie Robertson. He was a lovely lad, but he had a wicked sense of humour and I was concerned what he might tell the public and what stories he might weave.

I approached him standing at the bottom of the stairs leading from my office to the hump top. As I looked up, to my horror I saw the General Manager, Frank Patterson, and his wife, coming towards us. I just had time to beg Johnnie to behave and he just had time to assure me he would when they were upon us.

Introductions were effected. Mrs. Patterson said, 'Did you say your name was Robertson?'

'That's right, ma'am' replied Johnnie, the model of politeness.

'What a strange coincidence,' said Mrs. Patterson, 'my maiden name was Robertson'.

We all expressed mild surprise.

'I suppose you were born in Sheffield' she said.

'No I was born in Glasgow' replied John.

'Another coincidence!' she said. 'So was I.'

At that point the whole encounter took a nose dive. 'Hello Mum!' said Johnnie. It really was about the only time I wished the ground would open.

I was interviewing with Harry Whitehouse, a delightful gentle man, for the position of Train Crew Supervisor Rotherwood. The last interviewee had been Tony, another member of the MIC team.

I advised Harry not to ask any rules questions, mainly because I did not want to get tied up in knots by riders to the question. Harry agreed, but when Tony was sitting in front of us Harry asked, 'Tony, you're driving your freight train towards a red signal. What can you tell us about what you would do?'

Tony had been used to questions like this and immediately began to try and establish any other parts of the question that had been omitted but were relevant. As he questioned Harry, I began to realise that I had no idea what Harry was driving at - nor had Tony for that matter.

The process went on for about five minutes until Harry said, 'Come on Tony, you are driving towards a red signal - what would you do?'

'Stop' said Tony, very much tongue in cheek.

'That's what I wanted to hear' said Harry. 'No further questions.'

Tony and I exchanged bemused glances. He was appointed, however.

* * * * *

Tinsley also took in the freight operation in the Rotherham area and was responsible for most of the signal boxes. One box, Greasborough Road, was perched way above the ground and was therefore accessed by a very long flight of stairs. This gave the signalman good warning if he heard an inspector or manager ascending and he was able to warn those either side to follow the rules to the letter. The bell signals that were used were preceded by 'one on the bell' to call attention and this was acknowledged by the receiving signalman. It was common to miss the call attention off, so the word was passed when the 'chiefs' were about.

I was informed that one of the signalmen at Greasborough road had been reported as having a young lady in the box with him. I was staying in digs in Sheffield at the time, so I said I would pay an out-of-hours visit. About 19.00 I walked up the steps and for the next three hours, until he was relieved, I talked to the signalman - just he and I present. I duly reported the next morning that I had not discovered anything wrong. The signalling inspector said he would visit again that night.

He reported to me that he had found the young lady in the box and had suspended the signalman pending enquiries. Because of my interest, and because I had established a good rapport with him, I asked to see the signalman. He was very worried about what had happened and explained to me that his parents did not like the girlfriend and her parents did not like him, so it was the only chance of them getting together.

I asked him how long it had been going on and how often. He told me it was every shift he was on duty.

'Ah' I said, 'not two nights ago when I was there'.

'She was there' he replied. 'You remember you sat on the locker while we talked? She heard you coming up the stairs, got into the locker and stayed there quiet for the three hours you were there.' The locker took the form of a bench seat with a tip up lid.

At this point I let him off - I really did not have the heart to take the matter further. But we did have a discussion about other ways they could meet. It was the difference between wilful behaviour and a genuine mistake, and this should always influence a decision.

The chairman of the Masborough LDC, ASLEF, Pete, came to see me one day in a state of mild agitation. I thought we were in for some trouble but I would never have guessed the reason for his visit.

'Do you know John Smith?' (name changed).

'Of course' I said. He was a driver at Masborough.

'Well, he's outside' he said.

'Does he want to see me?'

'Yes' said Pete, 'but there's a problem. He's not John Smith any more, he's Patricia Jones'.

I didn't quite realise what he meant until he ushered in John, dressed as a woman from head to toe. John explained to me that he wanted to undergo a sex change operation and that the psychiatrist had told him he would have to become a woman in all but the physical side and only then would he recommend him for surgery. This phenomenon was almost unheard of then and I could foresee a mountain of problems. Some did occur when he used the ladies' toilets at Sheffield station and the female carriage cleaners walked out in protest.

He was very lucid and open about the issue and we talked for some time about how to manage the ramifications. My knowledge of the problem deepened as a result of his candour.

I saw him some years later on a train, now a woman in all but the law's eyes - it is impossible to change sex in the eyes of the law - and he came over to me and thanked me for my support and understanding. He looked very happy. He was accompanied by his boyfriend.

I don't think Pete ever got over his embarrassment, but John was a brave man. I can't think of a more difficult environment than Masborough train crew depot to live through such a problem, but it all passed off relatively untroubled.

* * * * *

Oscar Hartley worked in the Rotherham area. He was the

chairman of the NUR (now RMT) LDC in that part and was very left wing in his outlook. He was a barrel of a man, resembling the figure in the budgerigar cage who always returns upright after an onslaught from the resident bird's beak. I enjoyed dealing with Oscar for two main reasons: he was absolutely straight, and he had a wonderful sense of humour.

I had joined the Junior Chamber of Commerce in Sheffield and one of the projects I undertook was to compile a series of radio programmes for Radio Sheffield. It involved visiting local firms and interviewing some of the staff about their jobs. There was a programme called *Down your Way* which was similar and we wondered whether we should call it *Up Your Firm*. Luckily we were dissuaded.

I decided to interview some of my staff at Tinsley and Oscar was one. We also asked everyone to choose a piece of music they would like to be played, and Oscar chose the *Red Flag*. He added that if that wasn't available, *Matchstick Men* would do.

When it came to it, Radio Sheffield could not find a copy of the *Red Flag* and played *Matchstick Men*. I asked Oscar if he would make a fuss and we drew up a minute that explained his union were withdrawing all co-operation and would not even speak to me because it was obvious that I did not wish to have left wing propaganda associated with 'management'. The poor lady at Radio Sheffield was beside herself with worry and insisted on visiting Oscar to apologise and explain. I took her to a signal box where he was on duty. He played his part brilliantly, reminding me he would not even speak to me and accusing this unfortunate lady, despite her protestations, of bias etc. Eventually, with that delightful twinkle in his eye and his chuckle, he came clean. Normal services were resumed.

He also saved my bacon on one occasion when I was driving to a cricket match and was late. Glancing in my mirror, I saw the dreaded blue lights behind signalling to me to pull over. I got out, and before the policeman could speak I said I had just been called to Aldwarke signal box to deal with an emergency. All trains were stopped, and only I could save them. The policeman immediately said 'Follow me sir' and led me to the box car park, sirens blaring.

When we arrived he asked, to my horror, if he could see the inside of the box, as he was very interested in the railway. Oscar was on duty. As I entered the box, policeman in tow, I winked. 'What seems to be the problem? I hear you are experiencing multiple failures' I said.

Oscar only hesitated for a moment. 'Thank goodness you're here chief' he said. 'Can you go and crank the points so that I can start moving trains?'

As he said this he was putting signals back to red – safely, I should add - to stop movements. I thanked the policeman and said I would have to get on with it now; he readily understood and left. We restarted trains as he disappeared, and no harm was done. 'Thou wait for t'next LDC meeting' said Oscar. 'Thou owes me now!' I think I paid handsomely, but at least my licence is still clean.

Junior Chamber was an excellent society to join. It provided talks each week on various subjects and I became very involved with the Public Speaking Group. I broadcast a live quiz show called 'Top Twosome' on Sunday mornings on the Peter Crabtree (now sadly the late Peter Crabtree) show, which pitted the wits of couples against each other in a general knowledge quiz.

About half an hour before one show started I realised that one of the contestants was deaf. I realised we would have to write all the questions out and hold them up as I asked them. Then, to my horror I realised I would have to write the other side's questions also, as they would be offered for bonus points if the original couple couldn't answer them. Rule 1 - always do your homework thoroughly.

I was also allowed to 'drive' the programme, which basically meant operating that huge bank of switches which is set in front of people making records. The show was a phone-in and I had to speak to the caller while some music was playing and tell them that when the music stopped they would be talking to Peter Crabtree. Then I would tell Peter who was calling and patch them through at the right moment.

A very doddery-sounding man from Rotherham rang through and eventually I put him through. 'Welcome now to Mr Sykes from Rotherham,' said Peter. ''Allo lad,' replied the caller. 'What point do you wish to make?' asked Peter. 'I've been thinking o' this for sum time now and ma point is....'. The doorbell was heard in the background. 'Hold on,' said the caller, 'I'll be back in a minute'. Silence. Panic. 'Play some bloody music,' came through my earphones. We never heard from Mr Sykes again.

There were several very quick-witted people in Junior Chamber, and none more so than Terry Barker. Radio Sheffield sent Tony Capstick, their senior disc jockey, along one evening, and he also had a number one hit. He was a bit full of himself and someone asked him if he really meant some of the sugary messages he would read out on air.

'It's more the ridiculous names that I find laughable' he replied. 'I had someone ring the other day whose name was Brian Hollocks - what a name'. We didn't think it was too bad and were getting a bit fed up with him. Terry rose to his feet. 'Hollocks is my name,' he said, 'Brian Hollocks'.

* * * * *

One of the issues that has always interested me is helping the young to decide what they want to do as a profession. I therefore started a programme of visits from careers teachers from schools to give them a taste of what it was really like to be 'on the railway'. It was, I think, very successful and we certainly entertained a good number. Many of them sitting in my office would go green when they saw through the window behind me wagons apparently running magically under their own power.

Aubrey Morley, who by then had assumed the duties of Career Master at my old school, UCS, spent two days in the area and made the impression on everyone that I thought he would. All the staff, and in particular the trade union reps, thought he was an amazing man.

Work experience is a great addition to the curriculum for pupils, it should be obligatory for careers teachers too.

During my time at Tinsley the railway was undergoing a depressed period and one that was changing the whole nature of its business. As a result Tinsley yard began to wind down, and just after I left the Woodhead route closed to Guide Bridge, one of the four across the Pennines. This route was unusual in that it was powered by 1500V DC overhead lines and was one of the first, if not the first, railways in UK to employ regenerative braking. Basically, as the train brakes it feeds power back into the catenary, which is a very efficient use of energy. These were emotional moments for the staff concerned, as livelihoods began to be affected, with depot closures at Rotherwood and less work at the Yard. There have always been campaigns to reopen the Woodhead tunnel, and they will continue, but I fear it will be to no avail.

My time at Tinsley saw the death of Roy Calvert, who had had more influence on my railway career than anyone else. Roy had moved from Liverpool Street to Sheffield in 1976 and taken me with him in 1977. He became more infirm, if anyone of 42 years can be described as that, as he gradually succumbed to leukaemia. One afternoon Shelia, his wife, rang me and asked if I would go and see Roy in hospital, as he had asked to see me. He was asleep when I arrived and there was a jigsaw on his dressing table. I started to do it, choosing the less challenging parts first. 'Do the bloody sky first, not the easy bits' came a voice from the bed.

We sat that evening and talked of many memories and of my future. He told me to stay in operations because 'you'll make your name in that'. I have remained in the function my entire career and have never regretted it. After more memories and more laughter I left. He died hours later, a sad loss to the industry and a huge blow to his family and irreplaceable to me.

Roy was succeeded by Clive Durrant. He had worked with my father in Freightliner and Dad always said he was one of the brightest and best colleagues he had worked with. 'Never argue with him on a mathematical point' he advised and I learned why very quickly. He could do mental arithmetic in his head faster than anyone I have ever met.

I can remember the scene when he first visited Tinsley. He came and shook my hand, 'You know I worked with your Dad' he said. I told him Dad had told me as much.

'The sins of the father will certainly be visited on the son' he said solemnly.

In 1980, after three years, I saw an advertisement for Assistant Divisional Movements Manager, Bristol, in the Divisional Office. The area of responsibility covered an area from Gloucester to Penzance and up to Swindon on the main GWR route. I knew my father would be pleased if I worked on a real railway and I was keen to work off the Eastern, so I applied. I do not recall the interview.

On the day I arrived, almost literally, Arthur Catherall, the Divisional Movements Manager, had a heart attack and was off for about six months. This made me reportable to the Divisional Manager, and it was a difficult period through incompatibility.

MAURICE HOLMES

The culture of the railway of the 1970s and 80s could be epitomised by adjectives such as gentlemanly, honest, fair and incisive. Some may be surprised by the last one, but compared with the legion of ditherers there are today, it certainly was incisive.

Take those adjectives and apply them to a personality and you have Maurice Holmes. He always was, and still is, the perfect gentleman. He had a very sharp brain and was an excellent operator. He was always scrupulously fair and I never knew him become angry, except during the incident of the custard creams described elsewhere.

I first met him when he became Divisional Manager at Liverpool Street in the mid 1970s and I was lucky enough to work very closely with him when he was Director Operations at the BRB and I was his Operations Planning Manager. Maurice's outstanding attribute was his ability to direct quietly and unobtrusively. Not for him the front row or the push to be in the press photograph. He would ensure everything was in order and would then seemingly melt away, often unsung.

The problem with managers like Maurice is that in order to learn from them you have to work for it, and I think many give up too easily. The introvert, by his very nature, will not offer his experience easily, but if you hunted and found, you were the richer for it.

There was one occasion when I did upset him. Maurice was a staunch supporter of all things military and the law. For a time I was engaged on a study of the operating function throughout the railway, with the objective of removing a considerable number of posts. Whatever number I arrived at would of course be doubled by John Edmonds, then Director Provincial, so I had my work cut out.

The review had turned to the Board's operating department, under Maurice as Director, and I had discovered a group of four managers whose job was so secret that they could not tell me about it. They worked in the dark world of PO Box 500 and Royal Trains.

Since they would not tell me what they did, I recommended a 50% cut. On presenting this to Maurice, he was horrified. He leaned conspiratorially across the desk. 'Close the door' he whispered. I did so and his eyes flicked around the room, examining it carefully for listeners.

'I cannot agree to this' he said. 'In fact they need eight in the section, not four. I cannot tell you what they do, save' and he leaned further forward, 'they are involved in matters of high secrecy'.

As he spoke, a pigeon landed on the window sill behind him, peered into the room and cocked its head slightly, uttering a coo. I leaned further forward still, my finger to my lips.

'Shh' I whispered. 'There's a Russian pigeon just landed on the window sill and he's listening.'

I could not have made a bigger mistake. Maurice was not impressed and he let me know in no uncertain terms. The four staff remained, and strangely I became in charge of that department later in my career. Four remained throughout my stewardship.

Maurice was a great servant of the railway and I was lucky to have worked at the same time as him. He gave much and asked for little.

PAT HOWLETT

When I joined Crossrail as Operations Director I took over from Terry Worrall, who had been covering the job on a temporary basis. Apparently Terry had asked the PAs to lunch to celebrate Christmas and Pat was one of them. She expressed the hope that I, as the newcomer, would not be asked to accompany the party, and I was not invited. She became my PA and we became firm friends, so I have never let her forget that she didn't want me around.

Pat was fiercely loyal to me and the team. She would brook no criticism at all and defended us all with fervour. She protected me brilliantly from unwanted visitors and operated very much as a maternal figure to us all. Lunch would appear if I hadn't had any, and she was always most solicitous for my welfare. Pat enjoyed a good laugh and was a very sociable, amiable person.

The only people in the office who really suffered were those who had the temerity to use my mug. If I happened to mention that it was missing, she would gather herself together and set forth on a search mission like a galleon in full sail. I can only say that if she found the person who had inadvertently used it, that person would never even think of doing so again after the telling off that would be delivered.

Pat had one attribute which I do not believe to be well known – she could play the bagpipes. I can recall seeing her perform with a group in Chiswick. For a girl in London at that time, this was a fairly uncommon instrument to learn. One other little known fact is that she worked for Eric Segal, the author of Love Story who also, oddly, was a classicist.

Pat displays so many excellent characteristics, humour, loyalty, kindness, and empathy with people in problems - a real London lady. She has kept the group together since I left Crossrail and we have had many great evenings. I am glad the relationship continues - it would have been sad to have lost the company of someone so good.

HUGH JENKINS

Black floppy hair, trousers seemingly always at half mast, a gangling walk, slightly thick lips and a reasonably large nose; Welsh through and through with a delightful lilt. Enter Hugh Jenkins, who died far too early but who broke several moulds and attacked many shibboleths during his railway career.

Hugh became the Principal at the Watford School of Management, The Grove, which was run by BR. I attended the five-week middle management course there and became entranced by him. He was so very different. Slightly, if not totally, irreverent; a lecturing style that was energising and exciting and beat any lecturer I had experienced before or since; and a delightful use of humour. He made every subject fun and thus we learned far more easily. He was also a good snooker player, and a brilliant exponent of the art of liar dice. I did take up his challenge at snooker and beat him - not good for promotion - but he was untouchable at liar dice. He had a fabulous sense of the moment and would enter everything he did with great gusto, frequently laughing very loudly.

Hugh broke the office mould when he became Deputy General Manager of The London Midland Region. He had his office painted black and white and the cynosure was a chess set in ivory and ebony in the centre of the room.

I still have the report he wrote about me after the course at Watford and I am still touched that someone who was as dynamic and thrusting as he was thought well of me.

Hugh was a one off, certainly in railway circles. I suspect he would have been a one-off anywhere, and that was what made him so special – that and the fact that he was Welsh!

MIKE JONES

Mike was Chairman of the Young Conservatives when Edward Heath was Prime Minister, His vowels were as rounded as table tennis balls and he had no fear of walking where angels would not. He was also supremely confident, with a disarming smile and personality. I first came across Mike at Liverpool Street as the new operating assistant, grade MS1, under Mike's MS2 leadership. On one occasion I did question his instruction. 'Who's the senior man?' asked Mike very seriously and not without a little pomposity.

Mike, it has to be said is not one of nature's railway operators. Our office at Liverpool Street, Room 97A Hamilton House, overlooked the East Side of Liverpool Street, platforms 15-18 and in particular the junctions which allowed the parallel moves to take place. Mike would arrive in the morning and look studiously out the window. 'Peak seems OK' he would say with an air of authority. I didn't have the heart to tell him on frequent occasions that the moves were parallel but 45 minutes late.

One of his great attributes, however, is his ability to laugh at himself. He is so honest that we still laugh about an incident now 35 years afterwards. The incident was Mike's finest hour and involved the boat train in the down evening peak at Goodmayes. The train was declared a failure and stood in the Down Main platform at Goodmayes, full and standing, at about 17.20. Mike instructed the DCC that he had weighed up the options and was ordering a relief main line train to be stopped alongside on the Down Electric line and for all the passengers to be transferred.

In vain did the DCC and other controllers try to dissuade him, and eventually the arrangements were made. All passengers had to walk over the footbridge to gain access to the Down Electric platform.

Mike had, however, forgotten one very important element of the plan. All the passengers had luggage loaded in the guard's brake, and the transfer involved carrying innumerable cases and other assorted items manually over the bridge with the help of the one leading rail man who was on duty. The whole move took about 90 minutes. The chaos it created for the whole evening peak was indescribable and the incident was never forgotten. To his credit, Mike never tries to defend himself.

Roy Calvert never really understood Mike and certainly was unable to accommodate his political leanings. We were called to Roy's office one afternoon to be hauled over the coals following a particularly disastrous morning peak and to try and learn the lessons for the future. Roy was in full cry, a daunting experience, and we listened attentively. Suddenly the silence from our side of the table was broken. It was Mike, who was looking at his watch.

'Sorry Mr Calvert, got to go, tea with the Prime Minister.'

'Stay exactly where you are!' exclaimed Roy.

'Sorry' said Mike, standing up. 'Got to go, I have my invitation here.' Sure enough he pulled the official document from his pocket. Mike, to Roy's complete amazement, just got up and went.

'He's gone' stuttered Roy. 'He's bloody well gone!' We left Roy muttering to himself in disbelief. I do not know if action was ever taken, but if it was it would not have fazed Mike.

Eventually, having failed to gain the franchise for the Great Western, a project on which he and I worked, Mike started Hull Trains as one of the open access privatised railways and is flourishing. Good luck to him, he deserves it; the railway is richer for such characters.

CHAPTER 6

BRISTOL

When I joined the Bristol Division there were seven areas; Truro, Plymouth, Exeter, Westbury, Gloucester, Bristol and Swindon. The Area Manager Truro, Arthur Eplett, known as Rusty, was a Cornishman by birth and President of the Fowey Yacht Club. He lived in Fowey and knew everyone. Driving with him was a special experience, as his hands during an average journey would only touch the wheel for about 5% of the time. The other 95% he would be waving at all his acquaintances.

He had another problem. He was incapable of reversing, so we had to keep going. Put him in a yacht however, and he became a magician. He once steered us back into the harbour and stopped on the mooring buoy without ever seeming to look where he was going. He was a master mariner if I ever saw one.

Every year Fowey held a carnival. Through Rusty's network, which was extensive, the Red Arrows were persuaded to display over the town. The poster for the event announced all the attractions that were on offer and finished up with the words 'and a flying display by the Red Arrows'. Underneath that was written 'in the event of inclement weather these events will be held in the village hall'. Rusty always said he knew they were good, but...

Keith Lewis at Exeter was the practical joker. My secretary, Val, had married David Hounsell, the Traction and Train Crew Officer, and David, while driving on Dartmoor, had removed a large oblong piece of stone which he cemented into the top of his fireplace as a lintel. Keith obtained some headed notepaper purporting to be from the Druids' Association of Great Britain, and wrote to David saying he had removed the fertility stone and could he please put it back, as no more births would be experienced among the Druid community until it was restored to its rightful position. David agonised for days, until we told him.

The move to Bristol was a culture shock for me. The railway ran as it had done for years, it was like a time warp. All the signalling and traffic inspectors wore full uniform all the time. The Chief Signalling Inspector, John Forrester, ruled with benevolent discipline and expected and received the highest standards of all who worked for him, particularly of the signalmen for whom he had functional responsibility.

They reported to Hugh Leonard, Signal and Safety Officer, who in turn reported to me. The traction inspectors worked for Laurie Whitley, who also reported to me. These two men had given a lifetime of service to the railway and were extremely professional in their dedication and approach. I always found Hugh a little distant, almost as if he was putting up with me. He also made the fatal error of telling me almost every day how wonderful my predecessor (Colin McCeever) had been. That is never a good confidence booster!

When the Divisional Office was doomed through a large reorganisation plan, Hugh could never get used to it and spoke of the loss of the Divisional Inspectorate as 'taking away his pens and pencils'. I did not think he was right at the time, but I now realise how wise he was. We lost a whole layer of the most professional and knowledgeable railwaymen, on whom the operation of the network relied. It was a big mistake and I always regret not having seen the wisdom of Hugh's words and tried to put that view higher up the organisation with more force.

Arthur Catherall returned to work after about 6 months of my arrival. By that time I had been subjected to the management style of the Divisional Manager, who understood little about railways and employed tactics that would have made Genghis Khan blush. Bludgeoning through everyone and everything and insisting his way was right, he allowed no challenge. He systematically began to destroy the atmosphere in the Division and to strip it of its operational assets, whether they were people or resource. Arthur provided a good barrier between us.

* * * * *

As part of the modernisation of the railway, the traditional design of the level crossing had been changing over the years. Now gates were not obligatory; they had been replaced by half or full barriers that were worked off treadles or in some cases by the signalman. Some had their gates totally removed. The criteria for such an installation relied on the traffic movement of both road and rail, referred to as traffic moment. If neither were particularly busy, only flashing red lights would warn the road user of an approaching train and only a white light shown to the train driver would tell him that the red lights were operating satisfactorily. No gate was required. They were called open crossings.

It had been decided to convert Naas and Westbury-on-Severn crossings, on the edge of the Forest of Dean, to open crossings, and I was deputed to accompany the Railway Inspector, Lt. Col. Townsend-Rose, to assist him. The enquiry was necessary as part of the procedure, since it gave the local people the chance to voice their opinions. Most were against the conversion.

We arrived at Lydney Town Hall and found the room. In the middle of the floor stood an old collier - you could tell that from the tell-tale blue veins in his face- with a cloth cap perched on his head and a roll-up hanging from his mouth. Broom in hand, he was sweeping the floor.

Townsend-Rose surveyed the room. 'Where are we going to sit?' he asked me.

'Well sir, it looks as if they intend us to sit on the stage where they have provided water and glasses' I replied.

'I'm not sitting up there like some demigod' said the Lt. Colonel.

The collier looked towards us and asked in a very broad Forest accent, which sounded like music to me if we wanted the table moved. The Lt. Colonel made a fatal error.

'What did he say?' he shouted. 'Can't understand a word he's saying - is he a foreigner or something?'

I translated. 'He's asked you if you want the table moved.'

'Of course I do!' came the comment.

The collier eyed him. 'Well, move it your effing self then.'

The Lt Colonel luckily didn't understand that either.

During the enquiry a very concerned lady asked about the safety of removing the gates and the fact that to all intents and purposes the railway was open - possibly for her children to run on to. Vainly the Lt. Colonel tried to convince her of the record of open crossings and all other arguments in his armoury. Eventually, in desperation, he said,

'Look here, if you drive down the road at the moment and the gates are shut and you don't stop what do you hit?'

'Well, the gates' came the reply.

'Exactly!' he said triumphantly, 'And we have taken the gates away, so you won't hit anything'.

'Except the bloody train' whispered our collier.

The Bristol Division was mainly concerned with passenger

traffic, having the important centres of Bristol, Plymouth and Exeter as part of its responsibility. It did however, have a fairly sizeable freight business with china clay from Cornwall moving to the Midlands, mainly for paper making, and most importantly the Mendip Quarries, moving stone and aggregate to London for the boom in building that was going on.

There were also several lovely branch lines, none prettier to me than the line from Exeter to Barnstaple. The line passed through *Tarka the Otter* country and whatever time of year I travelled it was breathtaking. I had the privilege of accompanying William McAlpine around the Division on his former Great Eastern directors' saloon. This was a magnificent coach which we attached and detached to and from various services over two days, spending the night at Barnstaple. The coach had a veranda at the back and for part of the journey William invited me to join him, the two of us sitting in huge armchairs. The one thing that remains in my memory is the 'smell' of the railway - not at all unpleasant and very evocative of *The Railway Children* and other such films and stories. You literally smelled the countryside.

It was at this time that we introduced the 'open station' concept that is now so prevalent. The thinking behind the idea was to allow customers to board trains easily without having to search for their tickets to pass through a barrier that was manned by someone who would clip the ticket and allow them access to the train. The modern way is now to have an 'open station' or a gated one. Clearly there would be job losses and clearly there would be an increased workload for the on-train staff, who would have to check that customers were in possession of the correct ticket.

It was a difficult task to convince the trades unions, and I had the unenviable job of leading the negotiations. I have to admit I was never 100% behind the idea and when confronted with challenges such as 'how is the guard going to know who has got on a train intermediate station and where they are sitting so that their ticket could be checked?' I was not the strongest arguer.

Chester Long asked me on one occasion how we would be sure that customers would know that they had to have a valid ticket to travel. I replied that we would put posters up at barriers. Chester rightly pointed out that customers have selective tastes for posters and wouldn't read them. I said they would if the poster displayed the question 'Have you got your effing ticket'. Chester ventured that I was not taking the subject seriously!

One poor customer, on being asked for his ticket for the sixth time between Penzance and Paddington, suggested the ticket inspector 'keep the bloody thing' since he was clearly in love with it.

Eventually we introduced the idea, and though it was far better than the plethora of mindless people that we all meet at airports and produce passports and boarding cards at ever increasing intervals, I still believe that the right approach at the barrier such as Eurostar's is the better way of welcoming the customer.

CHESTER LONG

The trade union organisation within the railway was highly structured. At local level the LDC (Local Departmental Committee) held meetings on all matters affecting them. If there was a disagreement with local management it would be registered as a 'failed to agree' and referred to Sectional Council. The latter would also deal with matters germane to more than one area.

The Secretary to the Western Region Sectional Council was Chester

Long. A slightly studious looking man with a very broad Devon accent (he and his brother Spider were based at Exeter), he worked in concert with a wonderful Chairman, Ken Winter, who had the most attractive Welsh accent I have ever heard. I used to say to Ken that if he kept talking to me long enough I would agree to anything!

Chester was in charge of the committee, however, in the nicest possible way. He was fleet of mind and combined this with a disarmingly charming way of telling you that in his opinion you were a complete idiot. Offence could not be taken.

As with everyone I have met, I learned much. In Chester's case my main lesson came as a result of a dispute at Laira depot. The local staff were insisting that a chargeman shunter be placed at the outlet to the depot to regulate the trains into service. The Divisional Manager instructed me not to allow the post and I therefore ordered an enquiry, which, had I handled it properly, would have satisfied Sectional Council and we would have passed on.

I started the enquiry with the words, 'I have looked into this and am convinced that there is no need for the post.' Chester looked at me in disbelief as his carefully-laid plans disintegrated. 'How can you say that now?' he asked in that thick brogue. 'We haven't even heard the enquiry yet.'

He was right, of course. It was like the judge at the beginning of the trial telling the jury whether the prisoner was guilty or not - don't worry about all the nonsense of barristers and proof etc.

As part of my punishment we finished up one Saturday night observing the operation of the yard to see if it would be safe and efficient without the post. The other part of my punishment was to buy the fish and chips for everyone. Chester gave me a stern lecture, and I have never made the same mistake again. The chargeman's post was not established.

Negotiators like Chester trod a very difficult path sometimes. They formed the lettuce in the sandwich, with the bread either side being management and the local staff. It was fairly easy for management to make a determination, but if it was difficult to sell to the staff it would be Sectional Council who would have to bear the brunt of the criticism.

Chester always accepted that responsibility, he never shirked it. He was absolutely fair and ruthless with anyone who stepped outside the bounds of fairness and honesty. He did much good for everyone, and when I compare him with some of the more extreme and maniacal trade unionists who still exist in isolated pockets, I realise how good he was and how much he achieved for his staff through his enlightened approach.

SIR ALASTAIR MORTON

In 1992 I joined Eurotunnel as Safety Director, with the task of writing the railway rule book which would be used to supplement BR and SNCF rules and ensure safe running of the Eurotunnel system.

I had heard of Sir Alastair - who hadn't? - and I was aware of his reputation, though I never considered I would be much involved with him as he was more concerned with obtaining finance, whereas I was operational. How wrong I was! This amazing man had a direct and vast influence on my life, directly for the next ten years and indirectly ever since.

I was called to a Board meeting to explain the timescale I was proposing for the production of the Safety Arrangements which formed the overall principles of how the system would run. This document was divided into six volumes; Health and Safety arrangements; System description; Railway rules; Terminal rules; Emergency arrangements and Dangerous Goods arrangements.

I was a little nervous at attending what in effect was my first board meeting outside the nationalised sector, and was taken aback by the first item on the agenda. I was expecting dynamic, cut-throat debate among the finest brains. After Sir Alastair had opened the meeting, a Board member asked if he might make a point. He stated that he noticed that the paper provided for this board meeting was of an inferior quality to that previously provided and that the propelling pencils which had been supplied previously had been replaced by cheaper biros. He asked if the company secretary had decided on a new policy and that if so, could we return to the higher quality goods with which to make notes? The Board was assured that a return to the upper end of the writing materials market would be effected by the next meeting, and he settled back into somnolence.

I made my presentation, which included a brief description of the work to be carried out, and, more importantly, a timescale. Sir Alastair asked me if I intended to keep to the timescale. Surprised, I answered in the affirmative. Sir Alastair clearly took a note of all the dates, for he personally telephoned me on each one to ensure I was still on time. Thankfully I met my objectives. I began to understand why he merited his reputation, but I understood even more in the years that followed.

At the same meeting John Neerhout, an American working with Bechtel, said to me in a broad drawl 'Rich, you're going to meet people who are gonna get in your way and prevent you from achieving these dates - what'll you do with them?'

What made me do it I shall never know. 'John,' I answered in the same drawl, 'I'm gonna kick ass.' Silence; then the blessed relief of laughter. Did Sir Alastair make a mental note of me then? I don't know, but he certainly always spoke to me when he saw me and always appeared to have the time, a sign of an excellent manager.

Sir Alastair had the knack of turning up in the offices unexpectedly and would always be interested in all he saw around him. I very quickly learned some rules in interacting with him.

Do not read slides during a presentation. Use them if you have to, but as a prop only.

Never try and bullshit your way out of a question when you are unsure of the answer. Always answer 'I don't know, I will find out'.

Never submit a paper in which there is a phrase, sentence or concept that you do not fully understand. He would always find that section, no matter how long the paper was, and question you mercilessly about it.

Never allow yourself to be bullied (not that it happened much to me).

Never criticise a fellow director - he was intensely loyal.

Do not be overawed by him.

Understand what he wants and if you said you would deliver it, then do so.

Try humour - at the right times.

Make sure he knew that England were better than South Africa at rugby - only to be reminded now and again!

On his regular visits to the offices and later the operational areas, he was always willing to stop and talk. Certainly in the Eurotunnel control centre, when we were operational, he would come in and just sit and watch what was going on. The staff loved him and he deserved that affection, for he was a superb man manager.

He did not suffer fools gladly, as was demonstrated when he and I when to address a conference of engineers on the subject of Eurotunnel after we had both left the company. He had telephoned me to ask if I would help him out by describing the operation of the system, saying that while there was no money in it, he had asked for a case of fine claret to be provided as payment. This duly arrived.

At the end of the presentation, questions were invited. The average age of the audience was around 80, but one young man dressed in hippy attire with long hair and beard to match asked, 'Why did you spend all this money on building this tunnel when you could have spent it on saving the planet from destroying itself through not adopting environmental policies?'

I have to admit I was nervous for the young man's health.

Sir Alastair eyed him directly. 'I am surprised you are not wearing a long gown and sandals. Next question.'

At the end of the presentation and in the reception afterwards, he signalled to me and whispered in my ear, 'Get me out of here'. I feigned a telephone call from a Minister and received short shrift for disturbing Sir Alastair, playing to the gallery, but this was replaced with thanks after we had made our excuses and left. We spent a wonderful two hours sharing two bottles of wine - South African of course - and I listened as he took me through many of the challenges he had met in his distinguished life. He was also insistent that we discuss my career too - like my father, he was always interested in others.

Eurotunnel was a member of the international Conferences on Road and Rail Tunnels, and I had played a role in the selection of papers that were to be presented to each conference. When the conference held its biennial gathering and chose Granada as its location, I asked Sir Alastair if he would give the opening key address. He agreed and I arrived at the hotel on the Saturday afternoon prior to the Sunday 'opening'. At about 15.00 I received a call from Sir Alastair if I would like to join him and Lady Sarah for dinner that evening, and we spent a most enjoyable time with excellent food and good company.

On leaving the restaurant, Alastair, against his wife's wishes, suggested we walk back to the hotel as it was such a lovely evening. As we started he whispered to me, 'You know the way, don't you?' If he had known me better he would have known I often have a job finding my way home in the evening. For me, the satnav is one of the best gadgets ever devised.

We started out purposefully, but it soon became clear that we were lost and Lady Morton began to express her displeasure. Caution was thrown to the wind. 'If we turn left at the next road and then right the hotel will be in front of us' I said with as much confidence as I can muster. To my amazement the hotel materialised as I had predicted. Lady Sarah thought me amazing and Sir Alastair was sure I possessed magical powers. I just thought that if I could bottle that sort of luck I would be a very rich man.

When Sir Alastair left Eurotunnel he joined the Shadow Strategic Rail Authority (SSRA) as chairman. This was a body established by John Prescott, then Minister of Transport, to oversee the newly-franchised railway and determine policy and strategy for the future. Not long after this I was considered surplus to requirements at Eurotunnel and I contacted him to see if he had anything I could undertake at the SSRA.

It was most apposite that there was a need for some technical advice to the organisation, as it was peopled by very able staff but mostly non-railwaymen. I joined the organisation almost immediately on leaving Eurotunnel.

I was very keen to introduce Japanese ideas, culture (as far as possible) and technology into the British railway system and we often discussed the idea. An opportunity arose when Mitsubishi approached us with the idea of meeting their President, who was visiting the UK, and we accordingly set up a lunch in a private dining room at Mossimans.

The President of Mitsubishi is very close to God in the pecking order, and as we sat down to lunch and had all raised our soup spoons to commence the fare, he suddenly banged his spoon down on the table, followed in a nanosecond by the other Japanese.

'I want to say what a honour it is to meet Sir Arastair [sic] Morton, King of Eurotunnel!' he almost shouted. Alastair began modestly to thank him. 'No!' exclaimed the President, 'for me it is a [sic] honour!' He would brook no further debate on the matter. At least five times during the meal he went through the same ritual and hailed Alastair as the 'King of Eurotunnel'. I watched with amusement.

At the end of the meal Sir Alastair and I left through the revolving door. He went out in front where his car was waiting, but as he emerged into the street he turned. As I came through the door he grabbed my lapel. 'One word out of you, Morris and I will personally sack you' he said.

'But Your Majesty, I was about to open your car door for you!' I exclaimed. I was 'sacked' in forceful terms. Often when I passed him or entered his office afterwards I would reward him with a low bow and would be 'sacked' again.

Sir Alastair eventually left the SRA (as it had become) having tried hard to introduce 20-year franchises only. Chiltern was awarded such a franchise. He had wide-ranging ideas for the network and commissioned me to remap the franchises so that they looked more logical and were more efficient to operate. He tried to steer the SRA in a direction that was far more empathetic to the way the railway worked, meeting the resistance of senior figures like Tom Winsor, the Rail Regulator, who thought the railway ran on contracts and contracts alone and accordingly did much damage to the industry. Sir Alastair was totally disillusioned over the insistence of government that they would 'man-mark' the organisation and set up a 'cell' at No 10 to second guess what he was doing. The railway lost a great mind, while smaller minds remained and continued to wreak their havoc.

After I finished my 10-year association with Sir Alastair I heard from him only once more. When the accident at Potters Bar occurred, I spent two days on site. On arriving home my wife suggested I should listen to the answering machine. It was a message from Sir Alastair. He had landed from a cruise in Australia, heard the news, realised it was one of 'my' trains and had telephoned to say how sorry he was and that he was thinking of me. No more need be said.

When he died, a relatively young man at 62, a memorial service was held for him in Southwark cathedral. The building was packed to overflowing. Music reflected his passion for the National Youth Orchestra, of which he was Chairman. The words reflected a generous, humorous, highly intelligent high flier. If I had been called on to speak, I would have stressed his humanity, but above all his leadership qualities. I have never worked for a more inspiring or brilliant man.

GEORGE OLIVER

George was in charge of the telephone enquiry office at Paddington. Tall and bearded with a round, almost cherubic face, he was always smiling. Issues did annoy George, but he continued to smile. He was the starting point for many careers, since the office employed many junior staff, most of them in their first job on the railway. They needed a manager who was caring, avuncular, strict when necessary, knowledgeable and able to associate with the younger people – he needed a good sense of humour. Enter George, who was all of those things. What could have been a difficult office to manage gave me absolutely no problem. He did not rule by fear but by respect.

Because George was tall like me, we decided one day that we would recruit only tall people. The job adverts on the railway often had the phrase 'or willing to learn' inserted after a requirement. A classic would be 'able to drive or willing to learn'. We decided to put 'must be 6' 2''' or willing to learn'.

We interviewed an applicant on one occasion who had listed cricket as one of his interests. 'Who did you play for?' I asked. 'England' he replied. George and I took several minutes to recover, but it was true. He had been 12th man at Edgbaston, having played for Warwickshire 2nds and been called on to field during the test match. When he had gone out George insisted we appoint him no matter what. 'The Paddington cricket team is a bit light at the moment' he said.

George was one of few socialists who was not a socialist of convenience. He believed in the principles and he both practised and protected them - great fun to work with.

PETER PARKER

Our chairman was, of course, Sir Peter Parker, though his very manner obviated the need to use the handle. He was an extremely clever, affable man who demonstrated no affectation and positively glowed with warmth for his fellow human being.

Peter Parker was the start of a new culture within the railway. The old diehard railway broke with its tradition and appointed a chairman from 'outside', someone who was not a dyed-in-the-wool railwayman, the type that would swap war stories with the best, with added exaggeration for each time of telling. I do not recall any antipathy towards the personification of this change even before he had been encountered. If there had been, it would have swept away without trace when meeting with him face to face. Sir Peter had a phenomenal gift for putting all at their ease - of whatever standing - and was both charming and erudite.

My first meeting took place in my office at Paddington. He had not been appointed long when one Friday evening there was a knock at my door and round it came the slightly cherubic countenance of the new chairman. I sprang to my feet and introductions were effected.

'Would there be an office I could use to catch up on some work – I will catch the 17.20 to Charlbury?' he asked.

'You are welcome to use my office' I replied.

Sir Peter would hear none of it. He asked that I find him a desk somewhere and I duly obliged. I had been back in my office for about 20 minutes when I realised I had not offered him a cup of tea. On entering the area where we had installed him I found him chatting to Gladys, the messenger/tea lady, and there in front of him was a cup provided by her. He had found his way to Gladys' office and had already obtained his reward.

I accompanied him across the station to catch his train and rapidly discovered that in future I would have to start the journey from the office to the train earlier. He talked to every member of staff and every passenger who recognised him and wished to make a point. No one was ignored.

He did not just talk - he possessed those greatest of gifts, the ability to listen and to hear. Everyone received his full attention. This is not to imply in any way that he was a 'pushover' - far from it. He would give short shrift to those who misjudged his easy approach and thought he would agree with everything they said. But it was all executed in a friendly and totally non-pompous manner.

I had the pleasure of meeting him most Friday evenings and loved to discuss his acting days. I think he was a frustrated professional actor and indeed his son Nathaniel now follows that profession with great skill and talent.

A story that sums up Sir Peter's spontaneity and humanity refers to a time when, early on in his BR career, he visited Plymouth and was having dinner with members of the local community and railway staff.

Ken Hall, the area manager, had just completed 40 years of railway service and was about to retire. During dinner someone must have mentioned this to Sir Peter, and I understand he was annoyed that he had not been previously briefed about it. He called for attention and congratulated Ken on his achievement. He then apologised for not knowing of this earlier because he felt it right that such an occasion should be honoured properly. He proceeded to remove his cufflinks, which bore the BR double arrow logo and were made of gold.

'I was presented with these when I recently joined the BRB' he said. 'I would like you to have them to mark this occasion.' Ken just cried, and the whole event made a deep impression on all those who had been there or who subsequently heard about it.

I know that Sir Peter caused a different culture to sweep through the old rather fusty corridors of power. He had the personality to make that happen seemingly easily through his great humanity and philanthropy.

I have worked for more dynamic managers and possibly sharper ones, but I have never worked for such a fascinatingly thoughtful, urbane and empathetic man. He caused me to reconsider my approach to management. He was the only manager I have ever encountered who could be praised by someone who, when asked if they had ever met him, would say they had not. What a reputation. I would rather be remembered for those qualities than the mere results I had achieved or any monuments I had built.

FRANK PRIOR

I had worked with Frank's brother Ernie at Temple Mills. Both were keen union men, though neither could be said to be at the fanatical end of the spectrum. Both were fastidious in their record-keeping and both were blessed with the gift of excellent recall. They made formidable negotiators. Frank was the representative for the Liverpool Street control office and as the 'chief controller' it was my task to ensure the equilibrium was maintained.

125

Twice in my career I have worked with men who were ex-prisoners of war of the Japanese. Gordon Wilkes, Deputy Station Manager Liverpool Street, was one and Frank was the other. Gordon could not bear to be in the company of Japanese people, and on one occasion fled the office when a group from the Japanese railways arrived for a visit to Liverpool Street which had 'slipped through the administrative net'. Gordon just could not face them, so because I happened to be in his office, I took them round.

I do not think Frank was of the same mind, but he was most understandably and definitely affected. One talent he had perfected was that of Japanese art. He could draw in a most delicate and beautiful style, a subject he only discussed with me once.

I made a crass and sarcastic remark to one of the controllers in my first week in the job and it was Frank who smoothed it out for me and then gently told me not to do that sort of thing again. I am grateful to him for allowing that one mistake.

There was a position in the office to provide relief to the Deputy Chief Controller (DCC) and the Freight Controller. The DCC was in charge of the office on a shift basis and was the lynchpin of the division. It was he who made the minute-by-minute decisions, and I always welcomed the opportunity to 'sit in the chair' as often as I could. The relief position therefore was most important and, following interviews, I appointed Frank. His gratitude was touching, the more so that he had achieved the result through his own industry and approach and not for any other reason. He was simply the best candidate.

On being told of his elevation, he immediately informed me that he would have to buy two new suits. Frank was not prepared to sit in the Deputy's chair unless he was properly dressed. 'I must be properly dressed if the Divisional Manger visits the control office.' Whenever he was rostered to that position he always arrived in a suit, at other times he wore a sports jacket.

The fatal moment arrived when Frank was rostered on the freight job and the DCC went sick at the last minute. When Frank arrived I asked him if he would cover the DCC position. 'Only if I can go home to

Romford and change' he said. No amount of persuasion that his sports jacket was perfectly acceptable, particularly in the circumstances, would make him shift. Frank went home and returned an hour later. I covered the position in the interim. Luckily I was wearing a suit.

CHAPTER 7

PADDINGTON

The Station Master at Paddington is surely one of the most coveted positions in the early days and the heyday of the railway. It conjures up pictures of smart, moustachioed, distinguished gentlemen clutching top hats and peacefully surveying their fiefdom from No. 1 platform, confident that their authority is total.

Now it was me, albeit the Area Manager, who had assumed the role about which my father had once remarked, 'not only do you not speak to the Station Master at Paddington, you don't think about him without permission'.

The area took responsibility for the station and the line to Old Oak Common Depot inclusive. The engineering at the depot was the responsibility of the Area Maintenance Engineer but the operation, including Old Oak Common signal box, was mine. In all, including drivers and guards, there were about 1100 staff in total.

The major problem facing the area was industrial relations. Before assuming the role I had several conversations with the personnel department about how I should approach the job. I listened to none of them, preferring to make up my own mind.

The main protagonists were not, as was usual at that time, ASLEF but the National Union of Railwaymen (NUR). There were two LDCs in particular, the guards and the station staff. The former was led by a charismatic, highly intelligent, patient but driven man, Geoff Hensby. The latter, although ruled by Geoff, was run by the chairman, who was a trade unionist of the worst kind.

The crash scene at Paddington when the sleeper derailed

Presenting Robert Thornton, who supervised the restoration of the
royal waiting rooms at Paddington, to the Queen

Accompanying the Queen to her train

In charge of the royal train

Another encounter with her Her Majesty

Meeting Prince Michael of Kent at Eurotunnel. Christian Costa nearest the camera, Pascal Sainson behind him and John Noulton to HRH's left

With Her Excellency Aung San Suu Kyi at Eurostar, 2012

My father, the finest man I have ever known, in his Guards tie and blazer, aged 85

He had further endeared himself to everyone by taking elocution lessons to rid himself of his accent and adopted the accent of a retired colonel with a plum very firmly ensconced in his mouth. He was ignorant, rude and utterly ruthless.

Each week a committee had met at Regional HQ, chaired by the Deputy General Manager, Bill Kent, to decide how to deal with any issues and to discuss tactics. Orders to the previous Area Manager were issued and he was constrained through his instructions to carry out whatever had been decided. I announced that I would not be attending, since I believed such an apparatus would be too oppressive and allow me no latitude in my dealings with any emerging problems. I wanted to be my own man.

As an example of the tricks that were played, Geoff once told me he would ring me by the end of a specified day to tell me whether there would be a strike or not commencing the next day. He said it would be important that he could speak to me and that, if he couldn't, he expected the strike to go ahead. I recognised the tactic and told Trevor Morgan, Train Crew Manager to be prepared for a long evening. We sat in my office and, as I thought would happen, at 23.59 the telephone rang. It was Geoff, who expressed much surprise that I had answered. He told me there would be no strike. I know if I had not answered there would have been, and Geoff would have blamed it on the fact that he said he would ring me that day and I was not available.

I am proud to say that no strike due to local problems occurred while I was there. The only action took place on February 14th and was associated with a 'day of action' under the TUC banner. More of that later.

It is a reflection on the times however that when I left Paddington and proudly announced my strike-free record to the Chief Personnel Manager that he said I had clearly not been tough enough!

The area had the normal spread of assistants: Mike Phillips, operations; John Humphreys, commercial; Trevor Morgan, train crew; Ron Mclean, Administration and HR. In addition, because of our particular problem, Bob Stevenson acted as IR manager. The station was managed on a shift basis by assistant station managers, of whom Howard Jeynes was the senior and most experienced. Nothing flustered Howard, who always spoke in a measured tone. Each phrase was punctuated by an intake of breath in the form of a wheeze, which, unkindly, for it was an illness that caused this, was mimicked by many of the staff including, I regret to report, the Area Manager himself.

The other occupants of the post, Norman Walker, Mike Burke, Roy Mathews and John Cramp, all fulfilled their duties in a singularly professional manner and I was fortunate to be so well supported. I succeeded Don Gronow to the post, and he in turn had succeeded Paul Witter. The former kept himself to himself and was relatively popular, whereas the latter was not. I therefore had a good start. I was determined to try and build a team approach, which I believed was the route to a better-run area and a vehicle for sapping the power of the union stranglehold.

Services that operate from Paddington have remained much the same over the years: the main line to Bristol, Penzance and South Wales, the suburban services from Oxford, Reading and Slough and the local services to Southall, Acton and Greenford. During my time there were parcels and newspaper trains. The latter were operated at night, serving many of the same main-line destinations. These were loaded by the 'night gang', who consisted mainly of Greeks. When I first met them, they discussed me in Greek and were knocked sideways when I answered in Greek, thanks to my Classics background. I was a hero from that point on.

The station had 14 platforms, two of which, 13 and 14, were at the country end of the station next to the Metropolitan Line platforms. These platforms were served by diesel multiple units (DMUs) on local services. The main line platforms accommodated loco-hauled trains and HST's serving main line and suburban destinations. The famous platform 1 was open - ie no barriers - and there was still a magic about seeing a train off from that historical and much-photographed location, watched by the magnificent Janus-like clock.

A fairly new invention at the time was the main departure and arrivals board. It was of a dot matrix design and allowed for free-form text to be displayed, which was, of course, far more personable to customers. We used, for instance, to put the latest cricket score up when test matches were being played. Words, my father always said, are our only weapons and we must use them properly. I would usually find something I wanted correcting.

On one memorable occasion, an army lorry collecting post from the postal underground railway misjudged distances on the lawn and clipped the board. One of the supporting legs bent slightly. In a flash the operator had typed 'OUCH' on the freeform display.

During my time at Paddington, London suffered from frequent bomb warnings and some instances of bombs exploding, all masterminded by the IRA. All of us were counselled to be extremely vigilant and to keep a watch for anything suspicious. A report was sent in to me on one occasion that a man of Asian origin had driven on to the road that led from Praed Street, parked his car between platforms 8 and 9 and run back into Praed Street at speed, leaving his driver's door open. Police were called and a sniffer dog was employed. The dog went berserk at the boot of the car and the station was immediately evacuated. The Bomb Squad arrived and, using a robot equipped with a camera, gingerly made its way to the car and prised open the boot. We watched from the office with some misgivings. An army officer approached the car and waved us down.

The boot was full of marzipan. When we reopened the station, the owner of the car reappeared, only to be promptly arrested. He had been driving down Praed Street, seen someone he hadn't seen for years and while breath was being held in the station and butterflies were fluttering, he had been enjoying a leisurely coffee. The marzipan? He was a chef on his way to work!

It was the first time in my career that I had become involved with the commercial side of the railway. Paddington booking office took a huge amount of money and the enquiry office dealt with a large number of daily telephone calls to ask for information, reserve seats or pre-purchase tickets.

George Oliver managed the enquiry office and was the perfect round peg in the round hole. It was a good recruiting ground, so the average age of those working there was relatively young. George combined an avuncular approach with a hidden band of steel, which was ideal. John was the other way round. His principles were strong and his standards high; woe betide the booking clerk who stuck a label on the booking office window!

The location and size of the booking office were not ideal, and it is an interesting reflection on station design that those offices that serve the real purpose of a station are often overshadowed by the ancillary revenue earners. I particularly recall John Edmonds, during the fit-out of the new station at Liverpool Street, blowing a gasket when he discovered the police had an office which was prominent on the station and, in his view, should have been allocated to a shop.

Another example is St Pancras, which, despite its grandeur and stunning appearance pushes the Eurostar booking office into a corner to make way for a second Marks & Spencer, which has a larger shop further along the station complex.

A station is a station first and a shopping mall second. It must be designed and planned as such. In particular planners must take more account of requirements when things go wrong. Passengers need space.

London railway stations have their fair share of celebrities who pass through. It was my pleasant task to meet those who were advised to me, the most prestigious being the Royal Family. The Prince of Wales and Lady Diana were regular travellers and I also met Princess Margaret, Prince Michael of Kent and the loveliest of all, the Duchess of Kent. The staff at Paddington would queue up to carry the Duchess's cases; she possessed an aura and a beauty that was matched only by her lovely nature.

On one occasion late at night, the Prince and Princess of Wales were travelling on the royal train. British Transport Police were in attendance and I received a covert message that this was the last royal duty for a superintendent who had been on the force for 38 years. I was initially bemused as to why this should have been conveyed to me, until I realised it was so that I could ask the Prince if he would thank him.

The Prince got out of the car and I asked this favour, which was immediately granted. The Royal Party advanced on an unsuspecting policeman. He came to attention and saluted with such force that he knocked his cap slightly askew.

'Superintendent' said the Prince, 'I understand you are retiring'.

'Yessir'.

'What are you going to do?' It was at this point that the whole thing trundled down hill.

'Retire sir' said the Superintendent.

'Yes I know' said the royal personage, 'but what are you going to do?'

'Retire sir' came back the reply.

This script was repeated twice more until I decided to salvage the situation. At the time, the ex-Chief of the Metropolitan Police, Sir Robert Mark, was advertising tyres on television.

'Actually, sir' I interjected, 'he's got a job selling tyres on television.' The Prince looked at me as if I had taken leave of my senses. The Princess, however, understood the allusion.

'Oh that's good' she giggled.

We moved on and I could imagine the Prince saying afterwards 'What the bloody hell was he talking about, I said retired, not tyres!'

The Queen Mother travelled on one occasion on the Royal Train to the Cheltenham Races. I met her at the clock arch, and as we walked across to the train I asked her if she had any tips for the day's racing. I told her I had been asked to request a royal forecast. She was much amused and looked into her handbag for a piece of paper. She gave me the name of the horse and boarded the train.

As soon as I returned to my office I was bombarded with phone calls asking for the name, and the local betting shop took a large wad of cash from hopeful and optimistic punters. It had to be a good tip - after all it came virtually from the top.

The tip came in last - indeed it almost got involved in the next race. The next morning the royal train returned to Paddington bearing the royal, though now not quite so popular, royal personage. As the train stopped the doors to the saloon opened. There stood Her Majesty. She looked sadly at me.

'Mr Morris, I am so sorry' she said with feeling.

At 17.15 one evening I was informed that Sir Harold Macmillan would be travelling on the 17.30 to Oxford. This was a busy train and I immediately sent one of the supervisors, Ted Sereaton, to find and reserve a seat. I met Sir Harold, who was almost 90 at the time, and escorted him across the concourse to the platform. He was not very agile and the walk, which would have taken some time without breaks, was punctuated by him stopping to tell me stories and to show me his gold medallion, which he had as one of the only two surviving directors of the Great Western Railway. I told him that my father had served in the Grenadier Guards, which caused a stop of at least three minutes while he questioned me about Dad's service history.

Eventually we reached the train, now already about five minutes late. Ted had found a seat at the end of one coach, but Sir Harold refused point blank to sit there. 'It's over the wheels' he explained.

I walked to the middle of the coach, presented my card to the occupant of one of the middle seats and asked him if he would mind swapping with an ex-Prime Minister. There was no question and the change was made. Sir Harold gave Ted a 50-pence piece, which the latter initially refused. 'Take it and give it to your grandchildren' I said.

The generous commuter's 14-year-old son received an award. He was very keen on railways and I arranged for him to travel with the driver to Reading and back. Good outcome all round.

It was particularly interesting to me to see the other end of the spectrum. Harold Wilson, long after he had retired from politics and the office of Prime Minister, also travelled to Oxford. He stood alone on the concourse gazing at the departure board. There was no telephone call warning us he would be travelling - no advice at all. I had been at school with his son Giles, and as a result had met him briefly once or twice. I walked over to him. 'Can I help you, sir?' I asked.

He told me he was travelling to Oxford and I started to guide him to the train. 'Aren't you Richard Morris?' he asked. 'Did you study Classics at university?'

I have to say I was quite amazed that he could remember me and what I wished to do. We had an interesting discussion on the rights of Classics and the railways as a combination - I had to remind him he had studied History. Quite rightly he conjectured that there was more relevance to what he had done. I was struck, however, with the truth of the saying 'how are the mighty fallen'. Here was a man who had held the highest office in the land travelling on his own. He was not landed gentry and therefore did not qualify for the sort of treatment given to Mr Macmillan.

It was however the industrial relations that took most of my time. The worst time was during a day of action by the TUC, which I happen to recall was on February 14ᵗʰ. The call was for all affiliated staff not to work on that day as a show of solidarity with TUC policy. For the first time at Paddington, the instruction was given to all staff and some disobeyed. Some members of the station staff turned up for work.

The station staff LDC chairman arrived at Paddington in the afternoon, probably having consumed a liquid lunch, and when he saw that some of his staff were working he issued threats to one of them. The member of staff reported this to the ASM, who in turn reported it to me. 'Get him to write it down and I will do something' I said. Amazingly, he did write his complaint down, and at last I had some real evidence I could work with. I saw the chairman as he signed on duty the next day and suspended him from duty pending enquiries.

I issued him with what was called a Form 1 - the charge sheet- which he returned, saying he wanted a hearing. He asked to be represented by Mr Hensby and had an impressive list of witnesses. The hearing was arranged, and eventually it ran over two days lasting some 16 hours.

Many of the witnesses had been coached, but not very well, and had to be prompted by Mr Hensby. The whole issue revolved around whether anyone could prove that the chairman had threatened the member of staff. Mr Hensby triumphantly announced his last witness. Before inviting him he asked me a question. 'You have known Mr X for some time, do you think he is a truthful man?'

I had to agree that he was and was concerned, for he had accompanied the defendant on to the station that day. 'Are you prepared to say that if he says the defendant did not threaten anyone you are prepared to dismiss the charge?'

I had to say, backed into a corner, that I would.

Mr Hensby asked the first question. 'Did you hear the LDC chairman threaten the member of staff?'

Impassive answer: 'No, I did not'.

At this point I was concerned, but for some reason the Gods must have been watching me and gave me inspiration.

'When the chairman was with the member of staff, where were you?' I asked.

The witness stood up. 'If you imagine he was here, I will show you'.

Much to the bewilderment and consternation of Mr Hensby, the witness left the room and began to walk through corridors, doors and offices pausing sometimes to calculate. After about four minutes he stopped. 'I was about here' he said.

'So you did not hear him threaten the member of staff because you did not hear him - nor could you hear him - say anything? You were too far away?'

'Exactly.'

I sacked the chairman and the hearing ended. As I left the office at Paddington I walked down the stairs halfway along the platform on Platform 1. To my concern, I saw a large group of the station staff gathered at the bottom of the stairs. Perhaps a protest, I thought. One stepped forward and extended his hand. 'Best day's job you have ever done' he said. This was echoed by everyone.

The station was better for his disappearance and the IR situation was better afterwards. He took us to an industrial tribunal, but we paid him off before the hearing - it was worth every penny.

I experienced one nasty accident when at Paddington. The night sleeper from Penzance approached Paddington one very cold morning at about 06.00. The train hit the 20 mph crossover at the entrance to the station travelling at about 80 mph. The locomotive took the road into platform 8, its booked platform. Unfortunately it took it on its side, having tipped over as a result of its speed. The rest of the train derailed itself in the throat of the station and left a twisted tangle of carriage parts and rails. Thankfully, no one was killed and there were only slight injuries.

I was contacted - I was living in Chiswick at the time. As I arrived a little old lady was being escorted into the station. 'Are you all right?' I enquired.

'Oh yes,' she replied. 'I am fine, but I don't like being woken like that!'

Although there was some talk of the brakes freezing on the locomotive (a Class 50), I knew the driver had gone to sleep and I eventually persuaded him to tell us that this was the case. It was an interesting case, where the 'blame free' approach played its part. I could see that the researchers would spend a considerable amount of money to prevent something that had not happened. I told the driver that if he came clean I would not discipline him. He immediately told me he had gone to sleep. Vigilance devices were installed as a result.

I caused some amusement and amazement when I first arrived to view the carnage. I collected a radio from the office and walked down to the country end of the platforms. Looking at the damage and seeing the frosted ends of the sleepers, I spoke into the radio. 'Padd 9 to base'. In the office they were waiting for the call and answered immediately 'Base to Padd 9'. 'Can you arrange for a trolley of coffee down here, it's very cold?' Talk about sang-froid!

I also saw that we had one line available to us - the down main. I asked the ASM to arrange to run a service using just that line bi-directionally. One coach was lying at a precarious angle adjacent to that line and it was the general view that we would not be able to get past it. I squinted along the line. 'Plenty of room, 'I announced, 'tell passengers to keep their heads in!'. I was right by about three inches, and became notorious overnight.

Within two hours of the accident we were running into Paddington again - four HSTs per hour in and four out on one line. Can you imagine being able to do that now?

There was excellent liaison at Paddington between the British Transport Police and the staff on the station. Tony Clift was the superintendent and Alistair McQueen his inspector. The former was an enlightened policeman who never used his rank to appear 'above it all', while the latter was a very good policeman and a brilliant pianist. He arranged the music I wrote for my wedding and was organist and Best Man.

I had my scrapes with them. When the Regional HQ was moved from Paddington to Swindon, I asked the General Manager if I could retain something at the station from the old Regional Offices. I was offered three paintings and one poster from the 1920s, which I hung in the stairwell leading from the concourse to the office used by passengers who wished to make enquiries. Someone suggested I should have them screwed to the wall so that they would remain in situ. I asked the engineers if they would do just that.

I arrived the next morning to find the pictures gone. Not only that, there were some classic fingerprints climbing the wall and around the area where they had been.

I was furious. I rang Tony and asked for his best efforts at finding the perpetrators. Police arrived from every direction and much scene-of-crime work went on. The staff kept away from me that day, particularly the one who had suggested screwing them to the wall.

About 17.00 I received a call from the engineers' workshop. Could they put the pictures back now, they asked. To my horror I learned that they had taken them off the walls to measure and put fixings on and that they were perfectly safe. I rang Tony with trepidation. After 10 minutes he was still reading out possible charges.

We held a BTP open day at the station with a police car and a police response unit parked up on the concourse. It was a huge success and late in the afternoon Tony came up to see me. He sat opposite me, pushed his cap back, put his feet on my desk, loosened his tie and lit up a cigarette.

Outside in the corridor we heard the voice of Inspector Stevens: 'Come this way Sir, the Superintendent is in here'.

'Thank you,' replied the unmistakeable tones of the Chief Constable, Keith Ogram.

It is not often we are privileged to see a policeman move fast, but in one movement Tony sprang to his feet, flicked his cigarette to me, fastened his tie and straightened his cap. He saluted the Chief Constable smartly and introduced me.

'What are you doing here?' questioned the Chief. Tony, unusually, was lost for words.

'Actually,' I said, 'the superintendent was just saying that next time we will put a banner across the exhibition with 'British Transport Police' emblazoned on it.'

The Chief turned to the Inspector. 'What did I just say?' he asked. 'Next time' came the reply, 'we should put a banner up'. 'Well done Clift' said the Chief, and left. Tony was very grateful and since this event happened before the picture incident it may account for my lenient treatment.

While I was at Paddington, the Great Western Railway celebrated its 150th birthday. The celebrations culminated in the Queen naming the locomotive Windsor Castle at Paddington. In order that the station would contribute to the event we held an exhibition of railwayana. On platform 1, just to the side of the war memorial, is a door which has the royal coat of arms emblazoned above it. This is the site of the Royal Waiting Room, which was constructed for Queen Victoria and Prince Albert. The entrance from the 'taxi road' also has a door similarly adorned which leads into an octagonal room. To the left entering from the road was the Queen's room, to the right, Prince Albert's. The octagonal room served as a sitting/waiting area and led to the platform.

When I discovered the room, it was the kitchen for the buffet which used to be located there. It had large extractor fans and pipe work all over it and the walls had a fair amount of fat and grease attached. With the invaluable help of Robert Thornton, the railway architect, we restored it to its former glory and placed exhibits inside relating to the GWR. We did not charge entry but asked for a donation to the Woking Homes children's charity. We made about £4000. Some of the exhibits came from my own collection, and the Queen was very amused to learn that the First Aid certificate had been the one presented to my grandfather.

Rather cheekily, I asked the Royal visitors to sign the visitors' book, which they did with no problem. Anxious that it was not stolen, I detailed one of the staff to go and collect it. He was promptly arrested by the police, until I explained that he was acting on my orders!

I also devised the Great Western railway game, which was made by Gibson Games and, I think, sold reasonably well. We sold the game at the exhibition - all profits to the charity.

The royal waiting room is now the first-class lounge and still in use. Still in evidence too is the section of hand-painted wall covering that we uncovered when we stripped a small piece of paper off that had been put there in Edwardian times.

It was a great experience to be involved in these prestigious events. It is one of the great things about working in an industry like the railway - there is always something different going on.

* * * * *

The station throat at Paddington had a fairly efficient layout. The timetable on a railway as flat as Brunel's with much running at consistent speeds was fairly easy to operate. As with all termini, it was platform occupation that decided the service and the turn round time. During the layover the train had to be cleaned and reservations manually attached to the relevant seats. It was important to allow enough time for these tasks to be carried out, and it was these elements that decided the frequency of service that we could offer.

On one famous occasion, the regional office decided to cut the turn round times for High Speed Trains to 24 minutes. When one considers that trains from Penzance were undertaking a five-hour journey, there was every possibility that some incident could cause delay and that the already tight turn round time would be eaten into. The timetable was a disaster, and was quickly changed. As always there is a balance to be struck. It is perfectly permissible to reduce turn round time to the minimum necessary plus a little for contingency. In this way it is possible to save sets or to run more trains. As always however, the extremes do not work and on this occasion the plan was quickly changed.

Since there were still many loco-hauled services in and out of the station at that time, shunters were required to unhook the locomotives at the London end and hook on at the country end. Sometimes we would 'engine release' by pulling the whole train out of the station and propelling it back in when the original locomotive had been released.

The shunters worked to a roster which required them to cover platforms. This meant that, if they followed the roster, they would have to walk up and down a platform every time to perform the two duties. As with all good railwaymen they found a better way of working. One would cover the London end while the other stayed at the country end.

One fatal morning two shunters had a disagreement and one of them insisted he would follow the rostered way. In the mess room a fight ensued. The upshot was that one broke his arm, the other his leg. This was a most unusual occurrence. I was forced to sack both of them without hesitation. One accepted his punishment; the other took us to a tribunal for unfair dismissal. In order to tell the whole story to the tribunal, all the shunters were required to attend and they sat seriously in a line, all suited and booted. The case was, in my view, always going to fail, but it did provide a priceless moment.

It appeared that the fight started when one shunter picked up a very large glass ashtray and threatened to push it where it patently would not fit. His actual words were 'I am going to shove this up your arsehole'. What was strange as one shunter after another gave evidence is that they could all recall that phrase, and all repeated it with gusto.

The panel for the tribunal followed the traditional lines; legal chairman, trades unionist and a behatted Tory lady. At the end of the evidence the chairman said that unless there was anything else they would retire to consider their verdict. The Tory lady spoke. 'I wonder,' she said, 'if we could ask the accused to take the stand again? I really want to know why this fight started'. Everyone in the court knew why it had started and everyone held their breath.

The accused took the stand. 'I want to understand' she said, 'why this fight started. If I recall, you took an ashtray and said that you would shove it up the other man's…' and here she stopped and for some minutes consulted her notes. By this time I was bursting, as was the trade's union man. 'Ah', she said, 'arsehole!' with some emphasis. Pandemonium ensued and the panel left to consider their decision, which was in our favour.

* * * * *

The job at Paddington was another development experience for me. I learned much about industrial relations and benefited from the challenge it provided. I have to say that I never changed my way of working and could always, as my father often said, look myself in the eye when I was shaving. No compromise but a good helping of fairness.

Once again I met some great people and augmented my operational knowledge. It was time to move on, and an opportunity arose to work in a new company, Railfreight Distribution, which was formed to manage Freightliner and the wagonload business of the railway. I was appointed Production Director of the new company.

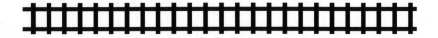

HOWARD REECE

Howard was a driver at Old Oak Common who worked the HSTs to the West Country and South Wales. He was one of the many drivers from Wales who had got their ticket at Old Oak Common, and he remained fiercely Welsh.

Howard was the secretary of the Old Oak Common drivers' LDC or local departmental committee, representing drivers who were mainly from the Trades Union ASLEF. He was a force to be reckoned with across the table. If I overstepped the mark, his moustache would bristle, his shoulders would square and his speech would became heavier and heavier with the Welsh accent, which of course I loved.

'Don't you come here telling me how to run my depot!' he would sing, almost as Owen Glendower might have done to the English army.

We once went to England v Wales at Twickenham. Wales won - to my chagrin - but on their scoring a try, things got worse. Howard was so excited he flung his arms round me and planted a huge kiss on my cheek. 'Bloody hell' he whispered, 'I've just kissed the Area Manager!'

As a driver his skill was supreme. He knew his job so well that he once drove from Exeter to Reading with his eyes shut - I hasten to add I was watching the signalling - and he hit every speed restriction exactly and speeded up again as soon as we had passed over them.

They don't make them like Howard any more – a cliché, but true.

FRANK SEEDS

'Have a mint', I heard, and a huge tin of glacier mints was produced. 'Don't think thou'll buy us off this time' said the union representative. 'But have a mint and let's talk on.' Negotiations with ASLEF, Tinsley, 1977, Frank Seeds style.

Frank was then train crew manager, and a great man to have around. Like Ken Britten, he had been a Chief Petty Officer in the Navy and would have filled Hollywood's bill as the cheeky chirpy northern Jack Tar, always laughing, always positive, even about his debilitating illness. Frank kept us all going. Even the ASLEF representative would give in and laugh at serious moments. The mints were Frank's tension diffusers, and no matter how many times he used the ploy, it worked. Part of the ploy was that you were not just offered a mint - it was placed firmly in front of you, banged on to the table. Luckily we all enjoyed them.

Frank had a sense of timing though. He instinctively knew when to quieten down and listen, and he attracted intense loyalty from his staff. Indeed, despite some of the difficult decisions we had to make, he was well respected by the drivers. Frank had one boss and it wasn't me but his wife Maureen, who worked in the Divisional Office. She was a calming influence. Slightly prim with a twinkle in her eye, slightly proper with a soupçon of wickedness, good fun, she was a caring wife to Frank. Frank became area manager when I left, on my recommendation. He deserved it and made a good job of it.

OSSIE SENIOR

Many of the staff at Temple Mills were West Indians who had arrived as part of the first wave of immigrants from those splendid islands. My abiding memory of them is the good humour with which everything was done, even in difficult circumstances. No one was more good humoured than Ossie Senior, a shunter whose job consisted mainly of coupling up wagons standing in the fans ready for train formation.

Coupling wagons using the instanter (a form of link) or screw couplings is not easy if you do it the proper way. Most of us used the buffer as a fulcrum and the shunting pole as a lever to lift the coupling out of the hook. The proper way was to engage the hook of the pole, under the buffers, on to the link and lift it to the hook on the adjoining wagon. The former method was considered dangerous as the pole, despite being ash, could snap easily (and did).

Ossie could have won an Olympic shunting event. I often walked alongside him as he coupled a train together and we discussed many topics in the easy, humorous way he had. As we walked, Ossie made the links dance, almost like a conjuror. He would flick the link using his wrists like the little master Tendulkar and it would miraculously jump straight on to the hook. He didn't break stride or conversation.

RON SHANN

At Temple Mills marshalling yard it was necessary from time to time to reload a wagon, either by adjusting a load which had become displaced, perhaps through a rough shunt, or complete transhipment, due perhaps to the original wagon becoming defective and unable to continue its journey - red carded, in railway parlance. This task was left to the transhipment gang, and the wagons were put into the cattle dock for their attention. The tools they would use were either muscle and brawn or an antique crane that Brunel would probably have recognised.

The leader of the three-man gang was Senior Railman Ron Shann. Ron stood out in many ways. Firstly, he never worked overtime and he never worked a rest day. Secondly, he arrived at 08.00 every morning in a Jaguar, which was ostentatiously parked on the cattle dock for all to see. Thirdly, he always carried a huge roll of £10 and £20 notes, interleaved with the occasional £50, which was regularly produced and from which Ron would carefully and deliberately peel a note for payment as required. Fourthly, if anyone wanted any gold, chains or bracelets, Ron was the man. He always had a fistful to show you. Fifthly, if you wanted a good breakfast in the morning the checkers' cabin was the place to go, and Ron would oblige. Sixthly, and sadly, if you wanted pornographic literature or magazines of any kind displaying anything you could think of, Ron's cabin stocked it.

Much wonderment was expressed as to how Ron had acquired his wealth. It was no surprise to any of us that his house was burgled. What was a surprise was the fact that he told me he had put his jewellery for safe keeping into cornflake packets, and only cereal packets had been removed in the robbery.

Ron was an amiable Bill Sykes, but as a result of the robbery, he purchased two Dobermans which would have made Sykes' dog Bullseye look like Lassie. I was introduced to the huge dogs when I visited Ron's house at his invitation for a drink before I left Temple Mills. 'Don't get behind me' advised Ron as I was greeted with two slavering maws attached to the most fierce-looking hounds I had ever seen.

Ron turned his back on me just once to pour me a drink and I could see the dogs looking at me as if I was a tin of Chum and getting ready eat both the meat and the tin. Luckily Ron turned in time to save me from instant death.

Ron did not die an old man, I have heard. There can be no doubt he was a rogue, but he exuded a certain charm. He reminded me of the character Noel Coward played in The Italian Job – the charming rogue.

IRYNA TERLECKY

I worked with Iryna at the Strategic Rail Authority. She was a lady who instilled a frisson of fear the minute you met her. She was not to be messed with, though you sensed a twinkling sense of humour and a fine mind. We had many conversations, because, like me at the time, she smoked. I have always found that smokers' corner was always a good place to catch up on gossip, and we shared many a Benson & Hedges together.

Iryna delivered the best put-down line I have ever heard. We were dining with some 'outsiders' and one of the party was particularly oleaginous towards Iryna, doing a fairly good impression of Uriah Heep.

'Terlecky' he said, 'where do you come from?'

'The Ukraine' said Iryna. Uriah then spoke in some unintelligible language, looking very pleased with himself.

'I said Ukraine, not Russia' said Iryna. Collapse of stout party!

ALF THOMAS

Each 'collection' of staff more than 50 strong was entitled to union representation through an LDC, local departmental committee. There were usually four members, who were elected by their peers. They in turn would elect a chairman, secretary and the other two and all would attend meetings. The LDC was entitled to two processes - consultation and negotiation.

Consultation was like marriage. My wife will tell me what she is proposing, but there is virtually no room for disagreement. She is telling me what is going to happen. There may be an opportunity to question around the edges, but the principle is set. Negotiation, however, is more open, ie when I propose something to my wife. There is a need to gain agreement on the issue, but if this is impossible then the matter can be elevated to a 'sectional council' which will try and resolve the point in question. The similarity with my marriage has already ended by this point, since I have no right of appeal to a higher authority - there isn't one.

The formula for what fell into negotiation and what into consultation was very detailed and would often form the subject of debate.

Alf Thomas was, when I first met him, the chairman of the Temple Mills guards and shunters LDC. He was one of the first arrivals of West Indian immigrants and spoke with a very heavy accent and a very quiet voice. The characteristic of his voice I recall best was a sibilance or whistle which occurred often as he spoke.

He was a formidable opponent in meetings. He possessed a sharp intelligence and was very quick on his feet. Mix that with one endearing quality which stood out in everything he did - he was very, very polite, and always a perfect gentleman.

Alf was promoted eventually to an Area Freight Assistant (AFA) at Temple Mills and it was said he was the first black man to attain management grade. I am not sure if he was the first, but he was certainly very early in the order. The staff at Temple Mills were none too keen on Alf being in charge, because there wasn't one dodge he didn't know and no wool could be pulled anywhere near his eyes. He was the perfect poacher turned gamekeeper.

Not only was he good at what he did, he was also very wise, and often I would turn to him for counsel in particularly difficult situations. He did not give advice as a management man but as a very good man alone, and that advice was always couched in clear and thoughtful argument.

After he retired he carried out some work for the Racial Equality Commission on how to integrate the races better. Knowing my interest, he came to see me with a questionnaire.

He asked me what I would think if I was driving through London and saw a white man urinating on the pavement. I expressed the normal disgust about the individual concerned.

'Now,' said Alf, 'same scenario but it's a black man. Would you be tempted to say how disgusted you were with black men - not just the one individual?'

Despite my hatred of any racial discrimination, I was forced to say that it would have entered my mind. Alf paid me the greatest compliment. 'I knew you would be honest,' he said, 'that's why I came to see you.'

I have long felt somewhat ashamed of my comment, despite Alf enjoining me not to, and I have tried ever since to persuade myself not to practise discrimination. I actually believe, thanks to Alf, I have succeeded.

Alf was a man who taught me much, always in a polite and gentle way. He was one of those men who I can readily say I am better for meeting. It was with great sadness that I heard he passed away recently. My only consolation is that I spoke to him not long before he died and had sent him the above words.

DENNIS THORPE

Temple Mills had two subsidiary yards when I was there, the East Yard and the Manor Yard (the West yard was open only for storage). The East Yard provided the marshalling area for local trips within the area. It was fed by a feed road, E1 in the main yard. Two or three times per shift, the East Yard pilot would travel to the London end of E1, draw the wagons down to the East Yard and reshunt them over a 'knuckle' (a mini hump) into the requisite roads in the yard. The selection of roads was controlled by a ground frame of point levers. Supreme among the ground frame operators was Dennis Thorpe.

It was, however, as a practical joker that I remember Dennis. His favourite trick was to wear a pair of hairy hands, purchased from a joke shop, whenever a senior official was visiting the yard. When I took David Bowick, Chief Executive, round the yard, Dennis worked the frame with a serious and concentrated look, wearing these gnarled and hairy hands. I had already had an experience with George Gladwell during the same visit and was now faced with explaining away another staff eccentricity.

Following a derailment on the main line outside the East Box at Temple Mills, I accompanied Mike Jones to the site and was met on the way by Dennis. Mike, ever the gentleman, stopped and asked Dennis who he was and where he worked.

'See that building there?' said Dennis, pointing to the Temple Mills wagon workshops. 'I work in there, curling the edges of the sandwiches in the canteen'. Another bemused official; another explanation. But it made the days go round.

CLIVE TUCKER

Clive spent 15 years as an engineer in nuclear submarines. I met him first at Eurotunnel, where he was a controller of all the electro-mechanical systems on shifts. I noticed one trait almost immediately - he never took his eyes off the screen when he was working; it was total concentration.

Immediately following the first fire at Eurotunnel I worked closely with Clive. He had been on duty that night and had taken action which, I am sure, saved the lives of the drivers who were travelling on the HGV train that had caught fire.

When we were reviewing the fire and what we could have done better, Clive suggested we visit the submarine base in Plymouth and learn from the Royal Navy submarine service how we should adapt our procedures to deal with such situations in a more professional way. It was a complete eye-opener for me. No one could fail to be impressed with the order and teamwork in a submarine, particularly during an incident. We transferred many lessons to Eurotunnel and became stronger as a result. My admiration of Clive's abilities grew and they have been proved over and over again in his careful and measured approach to setting processes, training and exercising.

Clive, like most Welshmen, is a keen fan of rugby. He is not, as most Welshmen are, a good singer. He is however a good colleague and a great friend.

NORMAN WALKER

Norman was an Assistant Station Manager (ASM) at Paddington. The ASMs operated on shifts and were responsible for the current management of the station. It was a job that ran to extremes. Sometimes it was maniacally busy, other times the station ran itself.

Norman had an incredibly loud voice. He told me that he could have been an opera singer, and I believe it. His voice was not only powerful but could cover great distances. He was a larger- than-life character who had the disarming habit of pacing around my desk when he was talking to me, slightly bent at the waist and using his hands in almost tai-chi manner. All this in slow motion.

He preferred the night turn and would always swop so that he could work it. He was the king of the newspaper traffic which was still heavy out of Paddington at that time. It was a world within another world. It had a language all of its own and traditions that took many years of association to understand. Trains could be held for the 'titles' if they made a good enough case, eg the presses had broken down etc.

Norman was all powerful. He could decide what people living in the West of England read in their papers. If he was feeling particularly left wing he could ensure that the Daily Telegraph and Daily Mail missed the trains, while if he was feeling particularly dictatorial he would let the trains go without the Mirror or Guardian.

One thing you always knew with Norman was where you stood. The phrase 'not suffering fools gladly' was written for him. He was an intensely proud man who did a very, very good job. He would brook no interference on his shift.

I once decided to try my hand at making a few operating decisions and took my radio out for a stroll round. After I had intervened on a few occasions my radio crackled.

'Padd 3 to Padd 9.' (Translated, this is ASM to Area Manager.)

Cheerful reply from me - 'Padd 9 receiving.'

'Chief - give me a ring on the land line will you please?'

I rang through.

'Chief, who's running this station, you or me?'

'You, Norm, of course.'

'Well f*** off back to your office and let me get on with it.'

Area Manager retired hurt but because of Norman's commitment, his personality, work effort and the fact that he was right, no further action was taken. A simple description - larger than life.

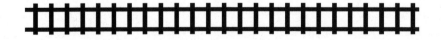

CHAPTER 8

TO FREIGHTLINER AND BEYOND

I undertook three posts in relatively quick succession over the next few years. The first of these came about due to the reorganisation of Railfreight. By the late 1980s the wagonload business was virtually extinct. Block load traffic was still plentiful, but it was decided to combine Freightliner, the container arm of the railway, with Speedlink, the residue of wagonload, which was moving not as individual wagon loads but as sectioned trains.

Freightliner had been an adjunct of the railway since the 1960s and its management did not take kindly to being 'taken over' by the traditional railway. It had developed into a far more commercially-aware company than the rest of the railway in the freight business and our arrival was seen by some as a retrograde step. To an extent they were right.

The company had many terminals dotted around the country. Containers were delivered by train to the terminals and delivered in many cases by Freightliner's own road fleet to the customers' premises, and vice versa. The major problem was that every customer wanted an 08.00 delivery, and that was impossible.

Freightliner operated their own terminals, their own infrastructure, including cranes, and a huge road fleet. Their terminal managers were a fairly independent bunch, as were the salesmen, who were divided into domestic, European and deep sea businesses. A challenge for the latter was the increasing size of deep sea containers, as large as 9' 6", which required infrastructure work on the railway or the development of small-wheel technology.

I think as a company we wasted our opportunity. There should have been a hearts-and-minds campaign with the new company and we should have moved forward in the development of the business in the excitement of innovation. It is fair to say that the new management did not understand the business well enough. Nor did we try to do so and drive the business forward.

There was a lack of a vision and a lack of a long-term plan. What should we do with Freightlinercare, the department that repaired containers? What should we do with the road fleet - retain it or contract it out? Were we ready for 9' 6" containers - should we invest in small-wheel technology? What should be the strategy with the terminals - we had several small and unproductive locations? Should we invest in swap bodies and save money on our trailer fleet? How were we going to cope with the 08.00 delivery syndrome? The list was endless, and very few answers were provided. I count myself just as guilty as the rest of the management group in not formulating a proper strategy against which we could measure ourselves.

Freightliner eventually flourished and today is a success. I have not followed its progress closely but part of the solution must have been a proper business plan.

As always there were some 'moments'. A resident of the Willesden area complained that his bed vibrated every time one of our trains left the yard. So persistent was he that I went to see him. I saw the problem immediately - it was a water bed and it rocked gently when the train affected the house foundations. It's the only time I have ever tried a water bed.

I pulled the winning raffle ticket at the Birmingham terminal annual party with the prize of a colour television. Much excitement, until I found it was mine and I had to redraw.

In an effort to build the team we went away to Arkelton in Scotland and tramped across moors, through lakes and over streams and rivers. On one occasion we were split into two groups, each with a radio, to maintain contact. I was one radio operator, Phillip O'Donnell the other. I tried in vain to call him. On return to base I asked him why he had not answered. I then noticed that the two radios were not on the same channel. 'Oh' said Phillip, 'I thought that was the volume control and turned it up because I couldn't hear anything.'

We met an amazing trainer at Arkleton. He had been a police dog handler; the dog's name was Odsall. Apparently Pete had used him at several events, fetes etc, where a 'prisoner' would run across a field and the dog would bring him down. Odsall believed this was for real every time and attacked the 'prisoner' with much enthusiasm.

Pete's friend, the 'prisoner', asked Pete if he could use a different dog. The first time this was done, Odsall was locked in the van and another dog was produced for the show. The 'prisoner' started to run, the dog was released and the commentator explained to the crowd what they were about to see. Then the commentator, with a surprised voice, since it was not in the script, announced that there were two dogs chasing. Odsall had apparently decided that he was not to be upstaged and had broken out of the van and set off after his canine colleague. The 'prisoner's' face apparently went ashen, and he recorded a time that was not far off the 100-metre world record. He was caught, however, and Odsall had his revenge.

There were some very able people working in the company and we did not integrate properly as a management team- all good lessons, however.

On leaving Freightliner I became Operations Planning Manager in the Operations Directorate at the BRB, responsible for the development of computer systems that would bring benefit to the railways. There was a small team of 'boffins' in York who were tucked away developing all types of programmes. The train service database (TSDB) was managed there. This and was for producing the GB timetable and was an animal before its time. It was a huge system which contained all train services and from which there were many bleed-offs, working timetable, station working books etc. The work there was relatively uncoordinated and certainly did not always reflect the needs of potential users.

I tried to change this and was successful to some extent, but I do believe that the whole concept of developing in house in this way was ill advised. What made matters worse was that other 'boffins' outside that department were developing systems which seemed to be more valuable to the industry. The team in York managed to stick its head in the sand while at the same time being at the cutting edge of technology.

I then returned to Anglia to set up a new regional HQ, making the sixth region. The railway by this time under the enlightened leadership of Bob Reid and had been organised under sectorisation principles. Each sector was a business with a bottom line - Intercity, Provincial Railways, Network South East, Freight and Parcels. Originally the railway continued to be operated by regions, although this eventually was passed to the sectors and the embryo of what the railway should look like was produced. Unfortunately Brussels became involved, with another meaningless mantra, and infrastructure was split out as a separate entity.

I am not sure of the underlying reason why the region was created. It is fair to say that Liverpool Street and Norwich were traditionally part of the Eastern region but were never really understood by the senior managers at York. Liverpool Street, in particular, was a very different type of railway and had not the time or the luxury of being beholden to the regional control. In addition I think John Edmonds was given a challenge because he was well known as someone who regarded the production departments with some suspicion - some would say dislike.

He was therefore appointed to create a new region to divide the Eastern into two with HQ at Liverpool Street. He interviewed me for the post of Regional Operations Manager. The interview went like this.

John: 'You know I have been asked to set up Anglia region?'

RJM: 'Yes.'

John: 'I need an operations manager. I am offering you the post. There will be no excuse for failure. You have 20 seconds to accept or not.'

I did accept, but it was nearly the shortest tenure on record. On the first Monday there was an exceptionally high wind. On the site of the old Shoreditch site above Liverpool Street, between there and Bethnal Green, piles of corrugated sheeting had been stored. At about 08.00 the wind picked up many of them and deposited them neatly over the catenary serving the six tracks into Liverpool Street. Chaos is not strong enough to describe the ensuing hours.

Mindful of John's statement, I offered my immediate resignation. An eyebrow was raised and the eye twinkled. 'Go and sort it out' he said.

It was good to return to my old stamping ground and I enjoyed being the 'boss'. We certainly improved the performance of the railway through grinding through the detail every day, which is what operations is all about. I recall sending out a telegram after a 100% right time peak that quoted A E Housman: 'Ten thousand times I have done my best and all to do again'. The involvement with sectors worked fairly well and the railway seemed to be getting on track. By combining Liverpool Street and Norwich it became easier to see the whole picture, and operations improved as a result.

Sectorisation of the railway was an interesting concept. The businesses all had 'bottom lines' and operated through 'contracts' with regions. The regions remained totally a part of British Rail, but there was a much closer relationship than there had been when the infrastructure was totally split from the train operating companies. We at regional level were very mindful of the priorities and objectives of each business and did our very best to look after them, and therefore their customers.

There was one problem however. It was becoming clear that operators were regarded in a poor light. We had almost become pariahs, and the future looked bleak I had one last opportunity to shine however. I was appointed Operations Manager at BRB, working to Terry Worrall as Director Operations.

I then became involved in some very different and very interesting aspects of railway work. The IRA was in the process of bombing London. Two bombs had exploded, one at Paddington, the other at Victoria. The second bomb killed a passing commuter. From that point on we were subjected to a number of hoaxes, which caused evacuations of stations and huge delays.

For three weeks we closed every London terminal on a Monday morning peak because a coded message had been received that there was a bomb at a London terminus. Clearly this could not continue and we, together with the BTP, instituted a series of comprehensive searches during the night so that if we received the warning again we could be confident that it was a hoax. The hoaxer stopped calling when he realised that there was no longer any point. He was arrested making a call from Kings Cross on week 4, after we had had the satisfaction of saying that we did not believe him any more.

One winter we suffered a very heavy snowfall. The snow was powdery and with the assistance of high winds it blew into the engine compartments of our locomotives and power cars, causing them to fail. Press and television reporters demanded interviews. Terry Worrall and I carried out over 40 on the worst day, trying to explain the reason for the problems.

The *Evening Standard* reporter who had interviewed us stepped into the history books by saying that we had called it the 'wrong type of snow.' He had fabricated the statement in a moment of inspiration, and the words have entered the language, even though we never said them.

As we took a taxi that night to get something to eat, the taxi driver spotted the billboard saying 'Railway manager says wrong type of snow.' 'What will the idiots think of next?' said the taxi driver disparagingly. 'That's your tip gone' retorted Terry.

It was, however, as Royal Train officer that I reached a childhood ambition. The Royal Train was used fairly extensively, particularly by the Prince of Wales. It consisted of several permanent coaches, to which others were added depending on who and how many were travelling. The Queen, Prince Philip and the Prince of Wales all had their own saloon, as later did the Princess of Wales. One of the permanent coaches was the train officer's saloon, complete with sleeping berth.

The arrangements that were required to run the Royal were time consuming and very detailed. Circulars were sent out on a need-to-know basis. A detailed plan of the formation of every train was produced and all personnel involved with the train were hand picked. The maintenance crew travelled with the train, as did a catering crew. I can recall even now the taste of the cakes the pastry chef produced - absolutely amazing. Mr Kipling would have been proud.

The train serves as an easy way for our royal family to travel, particularly overnight, out of the glare of publicity, and ensures that for a morning engagement we can take them to the location, stable them and allow a decent night's sleep before the engagement begins. It is also very secure.

I was lucky enough to accompany many of the Royal Family on journeys all round the country and even more fortunate, on occasions, to meet them in a relaxed atmosphere. It made me appreciate the delightful sense of humour of the Prince of Wales and the Princess Royal and I came to understand the pressures they were under, particularly those of publicity.

As the train officer, you were all powerful. Your decision was conveyed to controls as you were en route, and they were followed unquestioningly. But things did go wrong, some of which I am duty bound not to report. Others, however, I think I may relate without embarrassment.

One incident occurred as the train left Victoria with Princess Margaret on board, bound for Gatwick to meet the President of Italy for a state visit. I received information that Gatwick Station was shut, due to a bomb scare. If you are booked to go to Gatwick for such a reason you do not have many alternatives to consider.

I rang the driver and told him to slow to 30 mph in the hope that the scare would be cleared before we arrived. This of course would have caused some problem to the morning peak, but it had to be done. I rang the Princess' equerry on the train and asked him to let HRH know the reason for the slow running. As I had hoped, the all-clear was given and we proceeded on our way.

The equerry, a colonel in the Coldstream Guards, rang me in the office a few days later and asked to see me. I repaired to Buckingham Palace. The colonel asked if we could re-marshall the train so that his coach and mine were adjacent. This would mean that we could converse face to face if there was a problem and not by telephone, because the principal's saloon separated us and it was not possible to walk through.

I consulted the engineers and returned with two copies of the plan. I met the colonel in the Chinese Room where many years before, Fritz had proposed to Queen Victoria's daughter Vicky. He sat one side of the table with his entourage; I sat alone on the other. I began to explain the plan and he studied his copy.

I sensed that all was not well. 'Is everything OK sir?' I asked.

'You seem to have a different plan to me' he said. 'When you point to the locomotive, for instance, it's at the other end of the plan from the one on mine.'

I carefully picked up my plan and began to circle the table top where he was sitting. I placed it above his. He caught on. 'Got it' he said. 'Carry on.'

As my father remarked, 'you couldn't expect any more from a Coldstream.'

We had a problem with the costs of the train when the Government tried to compare the Queen's flight costs with those of the train. The flight was much cheaper –why did the train cost so much? Savings must be made!

It was not difficult however to discover that the cost of the flight was contained in the overall RAF budget and could not be separated. Therefore the cost of engineering, fuel, stabling, crewing etc was all 'nil' for the Queen's flight. Not surprising it was cheaper! The enquiries around Royal train costs gradually petered out.

The opportunity, just for a time, to be part of such events was exciting. I much enjoyed the responsibility, apart from one instance when we were stabled in Sheffield station. I was having a cup of tea with the station staff when a head appeared round the door. 'Thought I'd tell you, the Royal's on fire' it said.

Never have I seen railwaymen move so fast. It was a fairly small fire, easily extinguished, but it was the start, I am sure, of the grey beginning to appear in my hair.

Gradually the railway readied itself for privatisation and I found myself as Operations Director Network South East. The arrangements had not been thought through properly, and I have to say I found that time very unsatisfactory.

By chance I met Clive Durrant at a railway function. I moaned to him about the job and a few days later I was contacted by Peter Dyke of Eurotunnel and asked to discuss possibilities with him. I was offered the job of being responsible for writing the rules by which the tunnel would run.

I had to resign from BR to take up the post. John Nelson was the Director NSE at the time and on reading my letter, he looked across the table and said 'I cannot imagine the railway without you in it'. I was flattered and slightly emotional.

DAVE WARD

Dave is one of those admirable people who has worked his way up to the top from the bottom. Known around the railway as the 'Del Boy' of railways, he is afraid of no one and easily makes his views known through a combination of common sense and a huge wealth of knowledge. Fools are not suffered. Language can become blue. He often refers to his philosophy as 'wardie speak' and it is always worth listening to. His slightly rebellious streak appeals to me. My Father used to say when you met someone, 'Would you think if you were cast adrift in a boat with this person he would find a way home?' If that happened to me and Dave was on the boat we would finish up in some paradise somewhere, being looked after by the most beautiful ladies you could imagine. I regard him in the highest light. I love working with him even though as a union rep in a disciplinary hearing he completely caught me out. My fault, not his, I have been better prepared since.

JACK WATLING

When I first went to Temple Mills as a management trainee, Jack was a Hump Supervisor on shifts. There were many traps to fall into as a trainee and there were plenty of staff who saw the trainee as a threat because they would be 'fast tracked' and the railway still ran on 'seniority' as the reason for promotion. Such people would - never maliciously but intentionally - try and belittle the trainee, or make him/her feel unwelcome.

Jack was not one of those people. Throughout my time at Temple Mills as trainee, AYM, and latterly Yard Manager, he was the epitome of helpfulness and understanding. I always enjoyed my time more when he was on shift and I learned much from him.

I was a source of some embarrassment to him however, since in an unguarded moment I announced publicly that he reminded me a little of Gregory Peck. He was forever afterwards known as Gregory and inwardly I am sure cursed my indiscretion. He always had the good grace to laugh about it.

Jack was one of those unseen railwaymen who do their job week in week out to a high degree of professionalism and are not acknowledged as much as they should be. Perhaps this is right, for perhaps they don't want a public acknowledgement - just the satisfaction of a job well done. Jack certainly did his job well.

DAVE WINDER

I have often been heard to say 'Give me six Winders and I could run the whole railway'. This is a man who belies the present by insisting on the sort of standards that would have been prevalent 50 years ago in the railway.

Dave is a shy quiet man, and like many introverts it is always worth listening carefully to what he has to say, for it is always well thought out and always measured. He is one of those invaluable people who will not rest until a job is properly finished.

An engineer by persuasion, he told me once that when he had been an apprentice, his instructor had insisted that if a particular piece of equipment was held up by screws, all the slots in the screw heads must finish up parallel. This of course could be considered anal to an extent and it probably is. But the message and the standards such precision conveyed were the drivers to better quality and higher standards, and Dave is a man who expected and practised high standards.

As with other introverted people, sometimes others are impatient for answers and prefer the quick-fire discussion, of which Dave is not an advocate. Walking from the offices of London lines in Old Street to Cannon Street, I would ask him a question passing Moorgate and get the reply passing Bank. Experience taught me that the answer was always worth waiting for, so I waited.

It was immediately after the dreadful accident at Potters Bar that Dave shone. He and I discussed the repair work to the station as a result of the unit crashing through the London end and becoming lodged in the canopy. We were both insistent that we were not going to follow the railway practice prevalent at the time and take an age over the reopening of the station. We set ourselves a target of one week and even had to tell the railway inspector to 'get real' after he had suggested months.

Dave project-managed it quite brilliantly and at the appointed time, one week later, ready for the first train, the station had been completely repaired. Even the underside of the canopy where the rear coach of the train had become lodged had been whitewashed.

As I stood on the platform awaiting the arrival of the first down train, a commuter approached me. 'Was there an accident here last week?' he asked. Affirmative.

'Where did the train come to rest?'

'Just where you and I are standing' I replied. 'Bloody hell!' came the accolade.

Quiet and unsung, Dave just gets on with it; an operator of the best kind. The introversion is often belied by a wonderful sense of humour and an impish wit. Give me six Winders.

TERRY WORRALL

Terry to me is the ultimate professional. Small in stature he may be – and I have never ceased to remind him of that fact - but small he certainly is not in his ability to operate a railway and to manage people.

I met Terry sporadically through the first years of my career, but came to know him really well when I took the job of Operations Planning Manager at Board HQ and he was Operations Manager. We worked closely together, reporting to Maurice Holmes, who was the Director of Operations, a role to which Terry was appointed eventually.

My task was to drive through the computing development within operations as well as being responsible for the production of the infamous fictional Great Britain Timetable - GBTT. Terry was the Operations Manager for the railway and much of our committee work and operational work overlapped.

Terry has the driest sense of humour I have ever encountered. He is able to keep a very straight face and deliver lines and stories that are very credible. It is only much later in the conversation that you realise you have been duped by a well-honed sense of humour. Even his lovely wife Mary would testify to that.

Mention must be made of hotel managers in particular. Terry would brook no lessening of any standards. He was ruthless if anything was not to his liking and I believe that the suicide rate among hotel managers decreased dramatically when he retired.

He was caught out on occasion, such as the time when he boarded a plane on an internal flight in the US and berated a poor woman who was in his seat until he had reduced her almost to tears. Then he found out he was on the wrong plane!

We attended a course at Watford together which was made memorable, not by its content but by Terry's dismantling of the consultant running it, who thought himself to be 'top of the range.'

Our consultant told a joke at dinner. The Ayatollah Khomeini was travelling from Paddington and sat in a first-class compartment ready to leave when a gang boarded the train, entered his compartment and tried to kill him. The gang were all killed by the Ayatollah's bodyguards. This, said our consultant, only goes to prove you cannot have Shiite in the station.

The group at the table laughed politely. Not so Terry. 'Where was the Ayatollah going?' he asked. 'Why would he be sitting in a first class carriage? Richard, can you think where he could be going?'

'Perhaps to Chippenham to see Westinghouse?' I offered supportively.

'But what platform was he on?' continued Terry. 'How did the gang gain access to the train?'

Our consultant tried in vain to say it was just a joke. Terry acknowledged that, but insisted on probing the story and teasing out whatever he could, thereby completely destroying the joke, such as it was, and of course extracting much of the consultant's credibility.

Terry was appointed Director Operations following the retirement of Maurice Holmes and I was lucky enough to move into his old job and work directly for him. He was the most loyal boss I have ever worked for and I much enjoyed our partnership. He could be very definite in what he wanted and he always expected the highest standard of work and behaviour. He always got it - a measure of the man.

Terry had worked his way up from a booking clerk's position and had risen to the very top. It was one of the attractions of railway management that this was possible. Even in such a regimented, almost militaristic organisation, true talent was recognised and rewarded.

Early on in our working together the IRA bombing of London started and in that situation we worked very closely together and developed, I like to think, a healthy mutual respect for each other.

There are many stories that could be related about Terry and humorous situations but my favourite has always been the tale of the custard creams. Terry and I had been instructed by Maurice Holmes to find 20 posts in the organisation that could be culled. We had identified 19 and were stuck - until I realised that we had removed a senior manager's post but saved his PA. Terry did point out that the PA was also PA to another director, but I was sure we could work something out.

We delivered our paper to Maurice and as he read through it, tea and biscuits were brought into the office. Maurice had just bitten off a large chunk of a custard cream when he realised we had left a senior manager without a PA. To describe the reaction as an explosion is highly accurate. I was covered with crumbs as they shot from Maurice's mouth. We were summarily dismissed from the office to lick our wounds and the custard cream debris that had engulfed my jacket and shirt. Terry suggested that in future all issues should be measured against a custard cream scale - the higher the number, the more contentious the issue.

He made matters worse at our next meeting by offering Maurice a custard cream, suggesting they were very tasty. If Maurice did not notice me laughing, either he was slow on the uptake or I should have received an Oscar.

Terry became Safety Director at the Board and later was appointed

Managing Director Thames Trains only weeks before the tragic and dreadful accident at Ladbroke Grove. He was supreme at the enquiry and during all the publicity. It was ironic that such a professional and dedicated railwayman should have inherited the legacy, but such is life. I really do believe that if Terry had been appointed earlier, the accident would not have occurred.

One final thing about Terry which is a most important and valuable characteristic - he is always the same. By that I mean you always know where you stand with him. I shall count my association with him as one of the high spots of my career.

COLIN WRIGHT

Colin is not a railwayman. He was an airline pilot with British Airways, and that is where I first met him. I had organised a conference in London on safety and had invited BA to present, as I thought we would benefit from their experience of ergonomics and professional training.

Colin, as I learned later, was full of surprises. He presented a safety system which was called BASIS and used by BA. It was a fascinating use of the power of a computer which allowed managers to establish root causes of incidents and accidents. and I subsequently adapted it for railways, where it is still in use under the name COMPASS.

Colin arranged for a dream of mine to come true by taking me in the cockpit on a flight to Warsaw and back.

He was and still is the ultimate professional, with a wonderful way of talking in pictures. It was he that gave me a phrase I mentioned earlier, which I use regularly - always be at the front of the bus swerving when you see an obstacle, not at the back looking at what you have just run over.

He introduced me to the concept of blame-free management, which I totally embraced, and he taught me much about how to manage safety in a meaningful way that actually brought results. Not for Colin the monthly trawl through statistics that mean nothing. Not for Colin the grouping of all safety incidents together without hazard-analysing them. Not for Colin the often-heard phrase at meetings when someone is asked whether they have closed out an action - 'I am having a meeting next week'.

During the flight to Warsaw we were accompanied on the flight deck by the Chief Engineer of the A320 Airbus. We received a warning which neither Colin nor his colleague had experienced before. They set about understanding what it was, knowing it was not serious.

'Ah' said the engineer, 'I know what it is. I will repair it.'

'Leave it alone' said Colin. 'Touch nothing.' He turned to me.

'Never let the engineers fiddle. They will probably cause an even greater problem.'

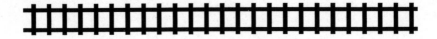

CHAPTER 9

EUROTUNNEL

It came as quite a shock to leave the mainstream railway, yet it was not a complete divorce, just a 'decree nisi.' It was, after all, a railway, and what's more it was a new railway with unique features that called for unique solutions.

It was made more complicated by having its own bespoke authority, the Intergovernmental Committee (IGC). It became apparent that SNCF had had the foresight to second its staff to the company, not so British Rail. If that was the route you had chosen with BR, it meant resignation and a new career.

I worked initially at Sutton and then transferred to the 'portakabin city' at Holywell. The site has now been restored to farmland, and where once we worked and ate, sheep now safely graze. The offices there were air-conditioned. This does not mean to imply a manufactured system; it was air-conditioned by the gaps in the walls and the roofs. Working there in the rain was a case of trying to find a dry spot!

The tunnel and associated systems, infrastructure and the rolling stock for Eurotunnel were all under construction when I arrived. The tender to build the enterprise had been awarded to a consortium of companies under the name TML - Trans-Manche Link. The relationship between Eurotunnel and TML could be likened to that of a nervous boyfriend (ET) meeting a possible father-in-law (TML) for the first time. ET was tentative, while TML appeared to me to exploit everything they could in order to put the price up as far as possible. Variation orders to the original design proliferated, causing huge hikes in the cost. In addition TML were, understandably, very hot on delivery from ET of the documentation and specifications that would allow them to deliver the system ET wanted.

TML professed to be very keen on ensuring that safety was at all times the prime consideration. The course I attended on site safety consisted of a reading from the Health and Safety at Work Act - not very inspiring.

I also had a problem with site access, after I had booked a film crew to film some safety points for me on site and one of the crew had a wrong name on the form. I asked if the session could go ahead and was told no. I waited for Jack Lemley, the TML MD, outside his offices and asked him if he could help me to continue the work. The answer was still no. We wasted £10k and the safety filming was not done until later. To my mind it made a mockery of their mantra that safety was all important.

One piece of documentation that was eagerly awaited by TML was the 'rule book', and that is where I came in. The overall safety arrangements were divided into six volumes: Health and Safety Principles; System Description; Railway Rules; Terminal Arrangements; Emergency Procedures and Dangerous Goods Procedures. The whole collection was referred to as the Safety Arrangements. Under these, as level two, lay the principles of each system or process. Finally came the third level, the detailed instructions on how to operate each system or process.

TML had complained that the rule book was late and that this was holding them up. Together with a delightful ex-SNCF lady, Christine Louise Lasbereilles, and originally under the direction of Dominic Daulmerie, I attacked the task to bring some order to the proceedings. Christine and I worked long hours to write the railway rules, hours that were punctuated by some fascinating professional arguments that occurred as a result of the cultural differences between our two railways. Christine was a very knowledgeable colleague and I much enjoyed the time we worked together.

Meetings were held with TML, fronted up by an old colleague of mine, Don Love, who had been Area Manager Liverpool Street when I was at Paddington. There was one memorable exchange between us when Don said that if things did not improve he would 'get contractual.' It was a tense meeting and well attended. 'Don' I said, 'you couldn't even spell it!' To his eternal credit he took it in good part.

The real problem area was, however, the Safety Authority. This was a committee of the IGC, and as its name implied it was the committee that would need convincing of our ability to run safely. There were some who understood what they were talking about - Pierre Defray and Claude Bordas from SNCF and RATP and my old friend Alan Cooksey, the railway inspector. The rest of the authority was peopled by those for whom bureaucracy is a hobby and whose knowledge of railways equalled my knowledge of medieval art.

The trick for them was to ask questions they did not understand and which were hardly relevant to what we were trying to do. They also trotted out a mantra - we need more information. When questioned as to what they required, they would answer - more information. They also had an annoying habit of telling us that the answers we had given to a particular question were not good enough and then refusing to elucidate, saying that was not their job. Eddie Ryder, one of the chairmen, an ex-nuclear inspector, was particularly good, and annoying, at this game. His French counterpart was nothing more than a petulant schoolboy who once told Sir Alastair after an argument with me 'I have never been spoken to like that before'. Alastair pieced him with a steely glare and said 'You'd better get used to it then'.'

Most annoying, however, was when one of the non-railwaymen tried to tell you what such-and-such a rule was on the national railways. That could be good sport!

We had a lot of help to put our documentation in order, not the least of which was from Tim Geyer, a consultant who worked with 4 Elements at the time and was a superb safety practitioner.

After a few months I assumed the role of Safety Manager for ET. I was able to introduce the concept of 'blame free' early on and to purchase the safety information system developed by British Airways, BASIS, which was adapted to Eurotunnel and called 'En Garde.'

One of the more difficult areas when constructing safety rules was the difference in culture to which I have alluded. We used to say that the French had all the rules and obeyed none of them and the English had no rules and obeyed all of them.

It became apparent that where rules differed, say in working at height, we had to adopt the more restrictive for our rule book. Thus we were forced to introduce restrictions when working at height that would be difficult to understand for one nationality, and we would have to line-test the catenary live before working on or under it, which was not the case in both countries.

Gradually the 'volumes' came together. The one that probably caused the most argument with the safety authority was Dangerous Goods. It is interesting that certain types of dangerous goods can be carried on a ferry but not in the tunnel. I can recall one meeting where I was told that the safety authority did not like the tense in which the document had been written - a very tempting discussion point to a classicist. I did ask if I should write in the optative – may you take precautions, etc!

We undertook practice exercises to test both our processes and our staff, and these were most useful. They have remained a very important part of operating a railway to me and are of much benefit. We were very lucky to have the knowledge and experience of an ex-SAS soldier who ran CPX's, Command Procedure Exercises. Since we did not have a tunnel or a railway we needed an alternative. Chris Goscomb, one of the most lateral thinkers I have come across, bought a selection of Lego and built the track, crossovers and all. Trains were individual Lego pieces and had to be moved manually to reflect the situation. The fun came when, on disengaging the train to move it, half the track came with it. We were good at re-railing!

The tunnel is 50 kilometres long and the deepest point is 45 kms under the sea bed. There are three tunnels, two running tunnels and one service tunnel, which is for the greater part located between the running tunnels. There are two undersea crossovers (where the service tunnel dives underneath or over the top of the running tunnels) which effectively divide the tunnel into six sections or intervals. All lines are reversibly signalled, which means that engineering work can take place in an interval and through single line working, the service can continue in the opposite tunnel, albeit reduced.

The track layout is very simple, being a figure of eight to avoid any 'changing of ends' in the terminals in Folkestone and Coquelles.

The service tunnel is pressurised by the NVS - normal ventilation system - which has the effect, when a cross-passage door is opened into the running tunnel from the service tunnel, of preventing any smoke in the running tunnel entering the service tunnel. Indeed, so strong is the air pressure that when a cross-passage door opens, a bubble effect is created and a section of clean air is provided between the door of the train and the service tunnel, thus allowing easy evacuation. An airlock at either end of the service tunnel provides the seal.

The tunnels contain drainage and cooling systems and a supplementary ventilation system which can be used to direct smoke in the event of a fire. Smoke and flame alarms are located along the length of the running tunnels.

Cross passage doors between the running tunnels and the service tunnel are situated roughly 375 metres apart.

Piston relief ducts (PRDs) which connect the two running tunnels are located about 200 metres apart and allow air to pass around the system to reduce air pressure. It is possible to close these ducts with a huge butterfly valve. This is done when work is taking place in one tunnel and provides aerodynamic protection to those working. If this were not done, the air movement in the tunnel under possession would be too strong for people to remain in safety.

Specially-built vehicles patrol the service tunnel, known as STTS - service tunnel transport system - running on a guidance system. These vehicles have detachable pods and can serve as ambulances, fire-fighting machines, people carriers or equipment movers. They have a cab at each end, a sort of vehicle 'push me pull you', as it is impossible for them to turn in the narrow space of the service tunnel.

At the undersea crossovers, huge doors are operated which seal one tunnel from the other. Of all the engineering in the tunnel this was certainly the most susceptible to failure. as they are very heavy and run on rollers

Four types of train use the tunnel, Eurostar as a through route to Paris and Brussels; freight trains, tourist shuttles carrying cars in single and double deck vehicles and HGV trains carrying lorries with their drivers accommodated in a club car at the front of the train. The latter two are operated by Eurotunnel and are lengthy trains, around 400 metres long. I always used to smile at the thought of the old BR rule that stated that the driver should walk round his train. Eurotunnel drivers have to be fit!

The rolling stock is provided with many detectors for smoke, fire, and petrol and each tourist wagon has a fire suppressant built in. This originally used halon. There was much disquiet about using halon even in a weaker mixture, as some thought it would endanger life. Sir Alastair offered to sit in a wagon and be subjected to a halon discharge to prove there was no danger. He changed his mind when I suggested I would be responsible for the cocktail quantities!

The railway was controlled from a purpose-built room at Folkestone. It contained a huge mimic panel, I am reliably informed the biggest of its time, which contained a display which detailed everything that was happening. Trains were displayed, along with the state of the ventilation systems, pumping capability and the status of the catenary and the crossover doors, piston relief ducts and cross passages. This meant that on entering the room it was easy to assimilate almost immediately what was happening. Trains were signalled from the room by the rail traffic manager (RTM) and the various systems in the tunnel were under the command of the Electro-Mechanical System Controller (EMS). The office was overseen by a supervisor.

A staffed standby control was available for immediate use in France. The situation now is different, in that the UK control room is now the standby, demonstrating the French bias of the company.

Alongside the control room was the Incident Co-ordination Centre. This was a purpose-built room which contained suites of desks allocated to police, firemen, ambulance and local authorities etc. Banks of radios were kept on permanent standby for the emergency services. Adjacent to the ICC was a small room with video and teleconferencing facilities, which was used a as breakout room where strategy was decided.

There were train crew depots in the UK and France, while the rolling stock was maintained in France at a building referred to as F45.

The signalling was an offshoot of the French automatic train protection system called TVM 430, which took the form of in-cab displays to the driver. The line was divided into sections and each section was indicated by a dumb marker, a blue square with a yellow triangle pointing to the line. The marker was dumb because it did not show an aspect - all that was in cab. The allowed headway was three minutes, allowing in theory 20 trains an hour.

Such a timetable would imply no differential speeds, however, and no slowing down at either end of the tunnels for the shuttles to gain access to the terminals. Eurostars travel at 160 kph, shuttles at 140 kph and freight trains at 100 kph. Such diversity is the bane of an operator and needs careful management to allow trains to pass unhindered. Effectively a Eurostar took up two paths. I did once suggest the simple solution of restricting Eurostars to 140, which would increase journey time by two minutes but increase capacity. This was greeted by a deafening silence

The system and the tunnels were a triumph of engineering. It was incredibly well thought out, and despite some teething troubles worked extremely well.

We did have a major problem on the day before we opened, however. We had decided to run free trips through the tunnel for shareholders so that we could test the system, on the understanding that it was at 'travellers' risk' if delays were experienced.

I received a call to inform me that a car had caught fire during loading at the UK terminal on platform 5. Arriving on site, I was struck by the unreality of it all; it was as if I was watching a video. A car had entered the top deck of the double deck shuttle, and as it was driving through it caught fire due to petrol dropping on to the exhaust manifold. The effect was dramatic. Smoke was billowing out of the top deck windows and firemen were arriving from all directions. Wishing to enter the shuttle on the top deck from the outside by ladder, they asked me if the catenary was isolated. Having checked, I gave my OK for them to enter the train. The fire was fairly quickly extinguished, although the instructions to activate the halon, which was suppressed during loading and required manual activation by the train crew, had not been followed.

As the firemen ascended and descended ladders a voice behind me said 'Have you earthed the catenary?' It was Keith Johnston, the overhead line engineer. To my horror I realised I had not and there was always the possibility of residual current being present. My look told him of my mistake. In an instant the earthing poles were applied which guaranteed there was no residual current and nothing untoward happened.

The overhead line is complex and requires dedication, an excellent knowledge and a high degree of professionalism. I have never worked with a better or more knowledgeable OHL engineer than Keith. He was someone I trusted implicitly. If there was a problem and Keith estimated an hour to repair, he was always spot on or thereabouts. He also had the skill of being able to impart his knowledge, and I learned much from him. We developed a mutual respect and trust – a great man to work with.

The fire caused problems, as the IGC chairman was apparently just about to sign our certificate to operate the next day when he received the news. Quite understandably he hesitated, and we had to open a week later after we had completed our enquiries. Poor Christopher Garnett, the commercial director, had to postpone festivities! Open, however, we did and I experienced a strange feeling of satisfaction and relief as I watched the first commercial service leave the platform.

By then I had assumed the role of Safety Manager and was

involved in many meetings with the safety authority to develop our safety rules. I also needed to introduce a safety culture within the company, and chose the principle of pro-activity and blame-free. I have described these in more detail in the chapter on safety and performance management.

An example of over-engineering, of which there were a few, presented itself when I visited the UK terminal control high above the lanes, where cars are marshalled awaiting loading to the shuttles. I noticed a pair of binoculars in regular use, the operator scanning the queues of cars occasionally as they were gathering to board. On asking what was going on, I was told that they were used to count the cars in each lane so that when the lane was full, further cars could be redirected to the next available lane. A remarkably simple piece of kit that was, to say the least, not expensive.

So far so good. What was rather less cost-effective was the elaborate system that had been installed, with under-lane detectors which sensed cars. When the requisite number were present it would automatically redirect oncoming cars to the next lane. It had cost a lot of money and had never been used. Motto? Always ask operators what they need, don't trust the engineer to provide it. It is a classic case of designing a totally unnecessary, expensive piece of kit because the user had not been consulted.

* * * * *

Once the system had bedded in, it became a fairly routine operation. The levels of reliability increased as we got to know the equipment better, and although the original concept for passengers was 'turn up and go' this was rapidly overtaken by a reservation system.

The business, however, was still being run as a project and desperately needed to change. By chance, Frank Esson, then of

Gemini consulting, made a cold call to the managing director to discuss if there was any opportunity for their change management techniques. Within a short time they were hired and brought a team of four or five consultants, skilled in different areas of change management, to work with a permanent team from ET.

I had expressed an interest in leading such a team and was asked to do so. I recruited all those staff whose managers said they could not possibly let them go and as a result I formed an excellent group. We spent six months on the project, initially being trained by Gemini in many techniques that have stayed with me to this day. We formed work streams and each change team member became a champion for a particular stream, facilitating the decision-making process with a team of on the ground experts.

We certainly started to change the culture, introducing a real 'can do' attitude. I can recall Mark Woodbridge, who was championing the introduction of Club Class, slamming his fist on the table in a meeting where those present were finding every reason why it would not open on the appointed date. 'We will open!' he quite simply remarked, and we did.

Xavier Bonneau, who had been the French terminal manager, was the son of a wine grower/producer. He was a very popular member of the team - for many reasons, I hasten to add. John Keefe was the deputy, although he disgraced himself by displaying the title 'Change Team Director' on a video we had made. All the team displayed a multitude of skills and we had a most rewarding and enjoyable time.

We removed £100m of cost from the business, changed many of the processes so that they were more efficient and introduced new aspects of the business. The only down point was a cricket match between the French and the English. The French won - I don't think I have ever got over that, nor ever will.

The change process is a fascinating technique. There is much science in the processes and programmes that are used and much art in the persuasion of staff to adapt. As always, some fell by the wayside, but overall the company benefited from our efforts.

All that was tested however when, at 02.00 on October 18th 1996, disaster struck. An HGV train carrying lorries from France to the UK entered the south tunnel with one of the lorries on fire. It was spotted by a French security guard in Calais who, as instructed, rang his supervisor, but by the time the control centre had been informed of the fire, the train was in the tunnel.

At this point the rule was to keep going, to get out of the tunnel. But as the train proceeded towards the French undersea crossover, a propping alarm sounded in the driver's cab. This was an alert that indicated that the propping carried on the loader vehicles, a bar that sat on the railhead during loading, had dropped and was in effect skimming the rails.

The rule for the driver was quite clear - he had to stop. What followed was some poor incident management, which nearly resulted in fatalities. There were too many alarms for the operator to deal with; there was uncertainty where exactly the train was stopped and opposite which cross-passage door; the supplementary ventilation system was not operated quickly enough, and communications left much to be desired. Luckily, as a result of the intervention of the ET duty manager, Clive Tucker, the disaster was averted and all drivers and crew were transferred to the service tunnel and safety.

The lessons learned and the subsequent changes made to the processes, rules and indeed culture are too many to elaborate on and would form a book in their own right. The main actions we took were a as result of a visit I paid to the nuclear submarine base at Plymouth. Clive Tucker, who had spent 15 years in nuclear submarines, and I were treated to professionalism of the highest order.

I learned the following: Collocate operational staff wherever possible; at the first sign of a problem configure systems so that they are ready to deal with an escalation of the incident; control the incident, don't let it control you; make sure your senior staff on call or in charge of a particular area of the operation are certified by the staff at that location as competent; use simulation as much as possible; drill, drill and drill again.

I moved to Operations Director following the fire and all the lessons were acted upon, increasing safety through a more professional management of incidents.

It was necessary, of course, to inquire into the events and during that period it was not possible to operate HGV trains. Within a week we were operating all other trains, but the interval where the fire had taken place was destroyed and it took many months to restore it. During that time our capacity was reduced through the need for single-line working.

The fire had started in one lorry, we believe through sabotage - there was a strike of the platform staff in France at the time - and had spread rapidly to other vehicles. It was not the firemen who put the fire out. According to an excellent fire expert that we hired, it was extinguished by a lorry of pineapples which literally consumed the flames. The same expert did cause me a problem when, at a very serious presentation to the great and good, he announced that in future all tunnels should be built from pineapples.

Naturally the negotiations with the safety authority to enable us to recommence HGV operations were long and hard, but six months after the fire HGV trains were rolling again.

* * * * *

We received many visitors to view our operation. Prince Michael of Kent almost caused my managing director to have a seizure. Having insisted I should be schooled in meeting royalty, he had to watch the Prince enter the room, walk straight over to me, shake my hand and say 'Richard, how lovely to see you again. My son did study classics following our discussion.' We had talked one day on the royal train.

'Do you know His Royal Highness?' said my slightly bewildered managing director later.

'I know them all, George' I replied nonchalantly.

A delightful admiral arrived to view the operation. When we took him into the control room, he stopped dead in his tracks.

'Mr Morris' he said, 'I want you to do something for me and do it now. That man with coffee on his desk - please remove it.'

The coffee was removed, much to the annoyance of the poor chap whose cup it was. 'On board ship once, major exercise' clipped the admiral. 'Chap on weapons. Spilt coffee all over computer. World War Three erupted, missiles everywhere. Frightful business.'

Pat Beaumont, an ex-colonel in the Paratroops Regiment, fulfilled an advisory role for the IGC on security and incident management. He was an extremely personable, slightly eccentric man who gave excellent advice, and from working in the diplomatic service he had a charm and persuasive ability second to none.

He organised for a group of high-ranking military and governmental officers from all over Europe to come to see how the tunnel worked and how incidents were dealt with. To that end he asked me, the Fire Brigade and police to simulate an incident which we would 'manage' in the incident control centre in front of the great and good. Because of the large number of observers, the group was divided into three, and we therefore had to play the incident three times.

After two simulations I became bored and suggested to Peter New, a high-ranking officer from the fire brigade, that we play the last 'show' a little differently. As the plot unfolded, I suddenly announced to the police inspector that one of the train crew had reported seeing a fox in the tunnel. Understandably his demeanour changed - this was not in the script.

'Not only have we found a fox, but it's foaming at the mouth' I added helpfully. The inspector muttered something that sounded rude and certainly included the phrase 'locked up'. Recovering himself, he quickly advised that the train would have to be brought into the terminal and the whole area quarantined.

Peter stepped forward. 'We know now why it's foaming. It's a dog fox and a female has also been spotted.' More muttering from the law, while behind him the observers wrote assiduously and unknowingly into their note books. Pat wore a puzzled expression. At the end of the exercise Peter and I just about escaped with our lives, let alone our freedom.

* * * * *

Eurotunnel was an exciting period of my career. The opportunity to work with French, Belgian and Dutch people was a thrill, and to become proficient in French was very satisfying.

We all had one goal and one objective - open the tunnel on time and safely. This common target meant the team worked hard and cohesively. When the tunnel was opened the pride at having been part of it was very prevalent. It still is for me, even now. But it nearly didn't happen.

On the day the Queen and President Mitterrand opened the tunnel, the incident control room was staffed. Ian MacGregor, British Transport Police Assistant Chief Constable, had asked that I be on duty because they were 'used to dealing with me'. It meant that my ticket for the opening ceremony passed to my father-in-law, for which he was eternally grateful.

The Queen's train, the Eurostar, had left Waterloo and all was quiet. On a police radio I heard the word 'bomb.' This was followed by a flurry of activity. I asked what the problem was. 'We have found a bomb on the line side at Marden' the senior police officer on duty informed me. 'It's a grey box with wires coming out of it and it is humming. We've just got time to drag it away and have a controlled explosion before the Queen arrives.'

I looked out of the window, thought a little and went over to him. 'Is there any writing on the box?' I asked.

'Why?'

'It could be part of the signalling equipment' I said quietly.

The order to drag the box away was rescinded, and sure enough it was part of the signalling equipment. Her Majesty would have ground to a graceful halt for a long time had the operation been completed.

I was told I could commit one crime in Kent and I would be absolved. I have not called in the favour yet. The ifs of history!

CHAPTER 10

PERFORMANCE AND SAFETY MANAGEMENT

During my career, mostly during the latter stages, there have been several seminal moments which have caused me to rethink my approach to safety management.

I have always believed that safety should be kept in perspective and have been concerned by those who seriously trot out the mantra that safety is always the most important thing we must consider. It is one of those apparent truisms that seem incapable of denial. Like so much else however, it has always been my view that balance must be achieved in all things.

Safety is one of the plates that have to be kept spinning, and one of those to which close attention must be given so that it is never allowed to start wobbling. A company could after all be very safe and completely bankrupt, because it had chosen to put safety first in all things.

On listening to the safety zealots, I often wonder if they check their brake lights every time they set off in the car. *Facta non verba* springs to mind.

One of the most important aspects of good safety management is to deal with the important or severe risks first. Therefore a classification of incidents into severe, medium and light is a prerequisite of good safety management. This means that a manager or a committee can use their time efficiently examining the most important risks, spending less time on the unimportant ones.

Management has only limited time and to concentrate on the

most risky events seems axiomatic, but practitioners are still often persuaded by the number of events, not the amount of risk. I recall a meeting at BRB where incidents concerning dangerous goods were under discussion. We had experienced a large number of overcharge incidents where the locomotive that had been attached to the wagons could not 'blow the brake off'. This effectively meant that until each wagon's brakes was released manually the train could not move. A video had been made to distribute to train drivers showing the correct procedure.

Hidden in the statistics were three cases of leakage of dangerous goods, and it was an eagle-eyed member of the meeting who pointed out that basically an overcharged train was at least safe, whereas leakage could prove to be a potential disaster. He pointed this out to the chairman, Sir Bob Reid. Sir Bob quickly announced that we had been spending our time on the wrong risk. Leakage, as he pointed out, could be far more dangerous than being unable to move a train. Our attention was rapidly refocused.

Good safety management implies capturing data that is risk graduated and ensuring that the high risks are dealt with as a matter of urgency. It is also important to use a number of measures of risk – not just historical data, but precursors and leading and lagging indicators.

The subject of SPADs has long occupied operators and safety experts. The acronym stands for Signals Passed At Danger, and clearly it is right that much effort should be expended on this subject. It is one of the most important principles in railway signalling that only one train should be in one section at one time, and a SPAD can break that principle.

As Operations Manager at BRB, I held a conference - and there have been many - to try and share best practice and knowledge around the railway to continue to reduce the number, and certainly the consequential severity, of a SPAD. There is a difference between coming to a stand just the wrong side of a red signal and passing it at speed (Ladbroke Grove) thereby running on into the next section with, sometimes, horrendous consequences.

Valuable presentations were made to the assembled group and much was learned. I had taken the opportunity to invite two senior pilots from British Airways, as I felt that maybe they could give some tips from their point of view about human factors or ergonomics.

In addition they presented a system called BASIS (British Airways Safety Information Systems) –they love acronyms too! - and although it was related to the SPAD problem it was far more wide-ranging.

The system has several objectives. It aims to present managers with the opportunity to understand root causes of accidents and incidents, the latter being often described as near misses. It analysed accidents and incidents into a matrix of frequency v severity and therefore prioritised management's efforts into attacking the most important events. It further contained an action tracking programme to enable us to make sure the severe events were being followed up.

Events were input using keywords and the power of the computer was used to mix and match keywords, under the direction of a manager, to pinpoint root causes. Was it always the same location in the same circumstances? Was the same aircraft always having a problem? Was there a particular period of time when an event was occurring, that was not immediately obvious?

The great difference between that system and more traditional ones was the analysis tool. Most systems talked merely of the number of events either rising or falling. BASIS gave the ability to use intelligent questioning and mixing of keywords through filtering to discover what was beneath the surface.

The pilots also outlined the 'blame free' principle of safety management, which decreed that if someone made a genuine error and said so, they would not be disciplined. If such a system is adopted it is clear that far more safety information will come to light and the real reason for an event occurring will be available, thus helping to ensure it did not happen again.

I found the arguments compelling. The short version of the story is that I helped to adapt the system for a railway undertaking and many parts of the railway use the system, now called COMPASS. I also embraced the idea of blame free against some strong opposition. There are still managers who need a stick with a rusty nail in it to maintain order.

What also was also powerful about this sort of safety management system was the gradation of importance of the risk.

The system makes it possible for managers to see what they are directly responsible for through assignment in the system and for all managers to receive 'reds' on a daily basis. This enables follow up of the most important events before tackling other, less important ones. It can also be used in real time during safety meetings to identify root causes and follow up reports.

Blame free is often misunderstood. The whole principle implies that if someone commits a genuine error and owns up to it, no discipline should follow. If there is a fear of discipline then there is no doubt that the incident will be covered up if possible, or if not, the truth will not be told and the real reason for the mistake will not be known.

During my time with Eurotunnel an incident occurred in which a controller livened up the overhead line during a possession. Clearly such an event could cause serious injury, if not fatalities. The controller immediately de-energised the line and reported the incident to the supervisor. Luckily no one had been hurt.

On investigation we found that the feed arrangements had been confusing, and this was the reason for the controller's 'error'. The arrangements were revised. The controller and his partner were given a weekend in London with dinner for being honest enough to report the incident. This was done in the knowledge of the blame-free culture. Their actions almost certainly saved a life – if the mistake in feeding arrangements had not been identified someone would have probably died.

What it does not cover is an unprofessional act, eg arriving at work under the influence of alcohol, fooling around in a dangerous manner etc. This caveat often causes confusion, because the adoption of a blame-free culture can give the idea that anything goes and no one gets into trouble.

If a differentiation between an incident and an accident is made (the former being effectively a near miss, the latter something which actually happens and results in damage to people, property or process), blame-free management should increase reporting of incidents.

It has been calculated that for every accident there are roughly 600 incidents. Loss of knowledge of these incidents will undoubtedly lead to a poorer knowledge of safety within a company. The more are reported and studied, the better the safety record will be.

There are some managers who would worry that because the number of reports goes up, the company must be more unsafe. This is ostrich mentality. It surfaced on one particular occasion in my career, when it was decided to abandon formal discipline if a driver misjudged a red signal and just passed it. Immediately there were more SPADs recorded, but I am sure the knowledge that was gained prevented a more major SPAD, which could have resulted in a serious accident.

There is an interesting formula that seems to apply to report and enquiry writers. It seems they believe they will be judged by the number of recommendations they make. Often they pay no due to the need to graduate their recommendations into those that should be immediate and those that can wait. How many recommendations gather dust on safety managers' and production managers' shelves, either because they do not understand them or because they are drowning in recommendation overload?

The ability of the system to filter facts in and out in a seemingly infinite number of scenarios helped us to understand real trends and therefore to spend management time on the real issues and not just the analysis that presents how many times something is happening.

The system, however, whether it is COMPASS or something else, is only part of the solution. The underlying principle is proactive management. Get ahead of what is going wrong and stop it. As Colin Wright, one of the pilots, put it, 'You want to be at the front of the bus swerving, not at the back of the bus looking at what you have just run over'. Later in my career, at Eurotunnel, I met a nuclear submariner who expressed it in a different way. 'You control the incident, don't let it control you'.

Safety meetings at all levels should ask at the end of the discussion 'Have we furthered the cause of safety in the company today?' How many meetings I have attended that grind through inane statistics, and how often have I heard 'We are still working on this, I have a meeting next week' as an explanation for inaction. Those sorts of meetings seem to concentrate on process and whether report (A) has been submitted according to this or that regulation or (B) has been discussed with one or the other departments.

Challenge is often seen as a potential threat, sometimes personally, as the recipient of the comment will end up in gaol. The debate on safety, if on no other subject, should be open and robust and result in a real, cogent, safer company record.

Knowing of a safety problem and doing nothing about it is dangerous. There must always be a process that should be used to attack the problem and reduce the risk. If not, there will be difficult times ahead when facing the judge. He will not be impressed by the event being under review. He will be even more unimpressed if there is no process to deal with a known risk.

As in all things, moderation must be exercised. There are so many stories, no doubt some apocryphal, of extreme measures being taken in the name of safety. No conkers in the playground and other such examples are well known. Such excesses do more harm than good to the cause of safety.

One major cause of safety problems is the false alarm. There have been instances in the airline industry where pilots have been misled into thinking that an alarm is false because 'it's happened so many times before'. This sort of culture will undoubtedly result in disaster. One very common example of the false alarm occurs on our motorways daily. Signs are installed at intervals along motorways which can either give just the speed restrictions in place or, in the larger signs, messages can be displayed. Mostly these are fairly fatuous - 'think bike' for example. Whatever does that mean, particularly to a foreigner?

However it is very common to see a sign saying 'queues ahead' and a 50 mph speed limit. Obediently, drivers reduce their speed and drive in expectation of seeing the queue. The next sign they encounter after a couple of miles is 'end'. There was some problem earlier, but someone has forgotten to turn the signs off. No matter, here comes another one, so we all slow down again. Once again, nothing. The third time, everyone knows it's a false alarm and drives on at full speed. This time, however, there really is a problem ahead, but the drivers are not ready for it.

The whole system of alarm management is also very important

to safety management. Usually the alarm system on a particular installation is designed by the engineer. The thought process must be something like - how can I make sure the operator of the equipment has notice of every system that exists? The answer is an alarm library. Usually there is no need to give the operator most of the alarms, and mostly it is written in 'engineeringese' which means little to the operator.

The first fire in the Channel Tunnel provides a good example. The operator in charge of all the electromechanical systems in the tunnel was faced with a succession of alarms which flashed before him one after the other for over a minute. He froze, and as a result did not carry out the full safety procedures. Luckily action was taken and the customers were rescued. The motto is - involve the operator early in the design process and ensure he is provided with what he wants, not what the designer thinks he might like.

Drilling procedures will help too. As a lesson taken from the military, the more a process or procedure is drilled or practised, the more familiar the staff will become with the actions to be taken.

Drills can be very short and sharp exercises, sometimes lasting only a matter of minutes. Announce a drill and the subject to be practised and ask everyone involved what they would do. As an example - the fire alarm has just gone off on the station. What are your duties to make sure evacuation is safe and efficient? There is no need to carry out the evacuation, though this can be done - merely make sure that everyone knows what they should do. Note down the exercise and who took part, and repeat as necessary, depending on the risk or the frequency with which staff are required to carry out the procedure. If it is rare, practise more. A simple technique leading to a more professional and confident approach.

Management by example and interest are good techniques to apply to safety management. Be mobile and discuss safety in an interesting way. If something is found and you have agreed to do something about it - do it. Nothing is worse than a broken promise. If, however, a safety situation is highlighted that you do not think is serious, argue the point and explain why you do not think it is worth the effort of taking some action.

Allied to this concept is the issue of professionalism. The railway has always been very procedural in its monitoring of knowledge of what we used to refer to as rules and regulations. All safety-related staff are monitored carefully and are required in many cases to take exams to demonstrate their proficiency. These exams are often biennial. When it comes to managers on call, however, the principle often disappears.

At Eurostar we have a process which requires all senior on-call officers to visit all locations at least once a year and be briefed by local managers. This enables the local manager to sign the logbook to say that they are content that the on-call officer is proficient in the elements they need to know. Each year the on-call officers take an examination to be able to remain on call.

At Eurotunnel I introduced a system borrowed from the Royal Navy, where the staff would pass the on-call manager out This entailed the manager being questioned by the staff on how the systems worked and what the rules were. This gave confidence to everyone that the on call manager understood exactly what he was managing. Just because someone is on call does not mean they are proficient. Leading by example means having to prove your professionalism, just as everyone else has to. Why would that not make sense?

The audit of safety is a key component of the process. Recommendations arising from an audit should be graded by importance so that they can be attacked in the right order. A system which quantifies the results, such as ISRS, is most useful, as it gives an indication of progress or otherwise since the last audit and shows the audited where they must improve. I have seen many audits and accident reports which contain recommendations almost into three figures, with no indication of what is important and what is not.

In essence therefore, make safety live; make it interesting; be proactive; adopt blame free and, most importantly, have a system which will help you to manage root causes and spend your time on the issues that really matter. If you go to a safety meeting, ask the question at the end - has this meeting made the company any safer? Limitless, meaningless charts will not achieve this, nor will information that just gives numbers of incidents. Spend some time thinking about what you are doing.

Performance management in many ways has principles that are similar to safety. An efficient system will ensure that good records are kept which allocate delay to the correct causes and which, as with safety, provides a system which allows managers to interrogate it for root causes. Once these are known, action can be taken.

In the modern railway, performance delivery falls under the responsibility of several companies. The infrastructure, the train, the staff, the stations, all could be managed by a different company. It is still prevalent to say 'the delay is beyond our control'.

The customer, of course, is not interested in that at all. The customer has been delayed and has paid the train company for his/her ticket. It is up to the company to co-ordinate all those involved in delivering performance and ensure they are professional and efficient in that delivery. They are primarily responsible. Rightly or wrongly, that is the situation.

The reasons for poor performance can each be allocated a number of delay minutes. This is not an exact science because delays – particularly secondary delays - can have several causes.

Nevertheless it is of little use to spend time and effort being over-scientific. The time and effort should be spent on trying to mitigate or eliminate the root cause of the delay for the future.

Because we have a measurement of delay minutes, it is also possible, by a leap of faith, to allocate a financial amount to each minute. Therefore, by estimating the cost of mitigating or removing the delay, it is possible to use a business case approach.

In addition schedules exist between the various parties in UK that result in money being passed backwards and forwards and netted out at the end of a month. The theory is simple - your fault, you pay; their fault, they pay. This can be dangerous on two counts. Firstly, such payment is not necessarily given to the customer. It normally finishes up on the bottom line of a TOC or Network Rail. Secondly, too much reliance can be placed in budgetary terms on partners failing and having to pay. I can recall a Financial Director once saying that Network Rail must be stopped from reducing delays because we, as a TOC, were not receiving the delay moneys we had budgeted to expect.

However it is important that a cogent plan is devised to find solutions to the more serious causes of delay. With a proper system - again COMPASS has a performance module - the root causes can be isolated, improvements found and costed and, if viable, they can be put into practice. The delay minutes attributable to that cause must be budgeted to reduce, and they must be monitored to see that they do.

It is of vital importance in the present fragmented organisation in the UK that the improvement plans must be agreed with all parties involved and that all should be involved in the reviews of progress. It is interesting to note that there is now a strong movement to combine the management of infrastructure and a TOC to drive better performance. Integrated controls are seen as the answer. I worked in one of those 40 years ago - *plus ça change!*

As part of this review it is important to revisit the timetable. Drivers are an excellent source of possible errors. A ride in the cab can be very instructive and I have often heard the words 'We'll be checked in a minute – we're always checked here because of xxxx'. A review of this type of confliction can often bring about easy changes. The review should include testing the point-to-point timings and where recovery time is inserted.

I can recall watching a rerun of a morning peak on GN using the signalling data and stopping the demonstration every time a train became two minutes late. We then questioned how that had happened and whether it was a fault of the timetable or just a problem of a failure or other late running. In doing so I noticed a ridiculous move that was made at one of our terminal stations where a train was transferred empty from one platform to another to free the platform for an incoming service. The shunted train usually left late. We removed the problem of the incoming train by some simple reworking, and the original train stayed in its platform and began to leave on time.

The audit of performance is most important. Any audit should be quantified and an audit that awards 'points' for the many aspects of performance management will be able to show, just as with safety, whether progress has been made or not. The most common serious causes for delay can also be covered by an audit so that, once more, the important reasons for poor performance are tackled first. I devised such an audit with John Mummery, then Regional Operations Manager for Great Western, and it has proved most useful.

The mantra around both safety and performance management is the same - to be proactive. If a warning appears, take some action to prepare for the logical sequitur that can happen as a result. Be ready.

There can be no doubt that performance and safety are linked.

Good performance equals fewer red signals and fewer staff on the track repairing equipment that has failed at an important time. A punctual railway calms everyone, passenger and staff, and leads to a more balanced environment. People are apt to make mistakes when operating outside the plan.

Nowhere is the adage 'plan, do, review' more relevant. A good accurate timetable, monitoring of the operation and good information to permit review; these are the objectives that should be pursued. Both safety and performance will benefit as a result.

EPILOGUE

My career continued through Executive Director, Strategic Rail Authority, Operations Director London Lines, Operations Director Chiltern Railways and Managing Director Crossrail. I thought at 60 I had retired, although I was full time on consulting. Then I was invited to join Eurostar as Director Business and Service Continuity and I am still in that post.

The railway has seen a terrific rise in patronage since privatisation, mainly through the release of investment and some more enlightened thinking on matters commercial. I wonder if technology will burst the bubble, certainly of the commuter railways, as I do not envisage commuters making the daily journeys in the same way in 50 years time. They will, as they already are doing, work more from home.

It has been a fantastic career for me and I have no regrets.

* * * * *

Peter Parker had ten commandments which he followed in business. Here are mine. There are some similarities.

1) Have fun and smile a lot.

2) Remember that people make it work, not things.

3) Position does not necessarily command respect - it has to be earned.

4) Walk and talk a lot.

5) You cannot manage people if you cannot manage yourself.

6) Remember the Greek motto, 'nothing in excess' - always keep a balanced approach.

7) Make sure you can shave in the morning, or if you are a woman, put your make-up on. Make sure you can look yourself in the eye.

8) Never compromise on honesty or professionalism.

9) Be worried if someone you don't like likes you.

10) Have fun and smile a lot (again).